Aj Woernicki's

Is There Love After PTSD?
Hope, Connection, & Freedom to

Be Who You Are

Featuring:

Alison Reynolds   Aly Shea
Randy Lynch   O.B. Wayland
Jamie O'Hara   Laura Bressan

Special Chapter on Sound Healing
by Laura Bressan

Cover Design by Liz Liano
with Aj Woernicki & Mariana Velykodna

ISBN 979-8-9907123-1-7

Copyright © 2024 Love After. All rights reserved. The names of some people have been omitted or changed. The names of the performers are as they are named on the individual creations. Any errors are of course mine, but still, no part of this ebook may be reproduced, or stored in a retrieval system, or transmitted in any form or by any means, electronic, mechanical, photocopying, recording, or otherwise, without express written permission of the publisher.

Table of Contents

Dedication 8
   Notes of Appreciation 8
Foreword 10
Preface 11
   PTSD and Me 12
      Anything Else? 13
      Is there love after PTSD? 13
   Families, Friends & Significant Others 14
   First Responders 14
   Healthcare Professionals 14
   Researchers 14
   How to Use this Book 15
   About the Writing Style 15
   Songs in the Text 16
   My Clearest Hope For You 16
Embracing the Trauma Journey 17
   Strategies 18
   Can this book help you? 19
   Why is this book unique? 21
      Why is PTSD different? 21
      What's It Like? 21
   Posttraumatic Growth 22
   A Note on the Research 22
      My Goals 22
      Why do you want to read this book? 23
1: Trauma's Mind Effects 24
   How does Research See PTSD? 26
   What Is Trauma? 27

- Where I Stand 28
- Understanding the Words 28
- How Deep Are the Questions? 29
- Changing Medical Definitions 31
- What Do People Talk About? 32
  - What's Different Here? 34
  - PTSD is a lot like a hurricane 34
  - DSM Advances 34
  - Autonomic symptoms 35
  - Dysphoric Symptoms 35
- The Biopsychosocial Model 36
  - Stories and Our Social Circles 37

2: Hello, Trauma. You're Me. 38
- My First Skydiving Practice 39
- Are You OK? No, but I'm Funny 39
- And Then What Happened? 40
- And What Happened Next? 40
- And Then It Began to Rain Down Hell 41
- So What's It Like Now? 41
- And What's It Really Like Now? 42

3: We Were Only Children 43
- My Story 45
- Reconfiguring 46
- Exit, Stage Left: How extreme … 47
- What's "Out?" Where's "Out?" 49
- Views From A Larger World 50
- The Music Born of Trauma 51
- Who Are We? The A Side 52
- Who Are We? The B Side 54

What "They" Say 55
4: Posttraumatic Growth 56
   Brother from Another Mother.................................. 57
   Creativity and The Great Escape 57
   Tears in Heaven 58
   What is "Creativity?" 58
   Courage, Bravery and Empowerment........................ 59
   Paradoxes, Losses, and Gains 61
   What is "Loss" in PTSD? 62
   The Broad Scope of Gains from Losses 63
      Gains and Losses 63
      Personal Development 64
      Physical Losses 64
   The Rewards of "I did this".. 65
   A Loss by Any Other Name.. 65
   Views From the Outside 66
   Views of Hope 69
   A New View ... and Results 69
5: The Maze of Edges 71
   Aly 73
      Rubies on My Wrist 73
      I saw that look... 74
   Randy 75
      Too Long Sober 76
      Haunted 77
   Orrin.. 78
      Pictures 78
   Laura 79
      Changing Flavours 80

- Jamie 81
  - Va-Va-Voom, or That's What I Say 82
- Alison Reynolds - The Back Cover 84
  - Back to You 84
- Clarity 86
  - Who am I 86
  - If You Aren't 87
  - Who am I – with you? 87

6: It's a kind of PTSD Magic 88
- (Untitled) Aly, 12/20/2023 89
- It Really Is a Kind of PTSD Magic 90
- Emotions are Not Feelings 91
- Emotions Are…? 92
- More than just words 92
  - How Fast is Fast? 94
- Making Connections 95
- What's the Magic? 95
  - The White Dragon: A Gentle Fiction 96
- How Did It Get So Bad? 97
- Inside Out 97
- Research Profile 98
  - Current Theory 99
  - A Wander to Finish the Magic 100
- Realities and Stories 102

7: Soundscapes of Our Lives 103
- The True Nature of Story 104
- Beyond Perceived Limitations 105

8: The Sound Walk 106
- So, What is Actually a Sound? 107

    My Journey To My Voice And Sound Healing 107
    My Sound Creation Process 109
    But what were my talents? 110
    My Personal Experience – The Sound Path 112

9: Ageism & Other Biases 116
    Sharing Crayons 118

10: Is There Love After PTSD? 120
    Emotions Aren't "Feelings" 120
    Is There Love After PTSD? 120
    This is a love story 121

11: Connections & Community 123
    Walking with a musician 123
    Resilience 125
    The Vast Scope of Connections 126

12: Ideas 128
    Chasing 129
    My Theory 130
    The Final Countdown 130

The Review Page: Was It Good? 132
Glossary 133
References 135
Index 139

Dedication

This book is dedicated to the two men who are most wonderfully, lovingly, and directly responsible for the woman I have become: Bobby (Gently so, my loving guide) and to a special man I met along the way who still doesn't know how phenomenal he is.

Brilliant musicians both, they are still "just men" in the most cherished sense of the word. Without both of them, this book would never have happened. Because I wouldn't have become who I am.

****

Notes of Appreciation

To Tauna, who was there in the beginning,

Thank you for the question about what I would want my readers to know: the story of my parents is about two people who settled; about how their hurts, disappointments and broken dreams painted a moving series of episodes full of sound and fury… it's a story of how your disappointments in life can become a full-blown something that you never wanted them to be

To Randy,

Thank you for your many contributions to this book, and thank you from the bottom of my heart for being a good friend and ally.

To Jamie,

Thank you for that amazing song "Va-Va-Voom" that reflects your own warm authenticity. And also for one of my top favorite lines in Songland: An Admission of Submission. And for all the times together… maybe even for talking me into this mess in the first place 😊.

And especially,

To Alison,

Thank you for creating this beautiful song, Back to You, and for letting me use it on the back cover. You didn't know me because you had already moved out of Cruces but you so generously allowed me to grace the back cover with your words. A lot of people don't know this but I am rhythm-dependent and this song was the grounding for the hard times.

It also tells Our story: We are lost, wandering, when we start and eventually we figure out that it's ourselves that we have to find.

Listen to *Back to You* with Paul Walter Kimball's soothing percussion on all popular streaming services.

And to

To Laura

And to Laura, for encouragement, the chapter on Sound Healing, and especially, for her beautiful song Changing Flavours that reflects the soul of this book.

****

"No. It's everyone. It's Bobby, who can still guide and kick my butt from the other side. Liam, who contributed both the love and the magic. Randy, who held me when I cried; Jamie, who just added so many fine details. Tauna, who gave me the lens to choose. Aly, Alex, Orrin, Liz, Alison, you, - all people who contributed songs, insight, solace for woe, gems of wisdom and delight..." (Chat with Chuck Sutherland, 3/8/2024.)

****

And also to The Starchild, whose sheer courage and determinism have inspired me in ways I never would have imagined when I began writing this book: my heartfelt thanks and deepest gratitude.

****

And I would like to thank ALL my friends for their love and support, for proofreading, for asking questions and Influencing the direction of this book.

And to those who offered up their stories that others might understand, I salute you. And then I hug you.

Foreword

Aj Woernicki has written a compelling, mindful, informative, and touching book about PTSD that I recommend for both trauma survivors and trauma therapists alike.

I found this book to be bravely and personally written as Aj explores and presents her own deeply wounding past traumatic experiences throughout. Aj, a singer/songwriter, artistically incorporates lyrics from her songs and from the lyrics of fellow trauma experiencers and songwriter friends to illustrate her perspective and the sound neurological and psychological facts she writes about. I find the use of these lyrics to be a lovely addition that enhances many of her points and personal stories. As a trauma therapist, singer/songwriter, and a trauma survivor myself (although I dislike the "survivor" handle but as of yet haven't really found a better one), I appreciate her sound research into the theory and practice of trauma therapy as practiced here and now, and find her present information is as up to date as possible with our ever-evolving profession and treatment modalities.

Having been a psychotherapist specializing in PTSD for well over 30 years, I found this book to be interestingly comparable to Alice Millers' world-renowned work, "The Drama of the Gifted Child", but more compelling due to its being courageously written from the author's own trauma experiences as she delves into a deep exploration of the "gifts" that experiencers of PTSD can access and may uncover as they heal in the form of deep, soul touching creativity. Aj uses the phase "Posttraumatic Growth," which relates aptly to the creativity the healing of trauma wounds often release.

It was an honor and a privilege to review this beautifully written, very personal yet informative book that I am sure will help many.

Debra J Antari, MS, LPC
Psychotherapist, Singer/Songwriter, Healer

Preface

Living with PTSD is like living with a not-so-imaginary but still invisible friend. This friend doesn't exactly live inside you but it doesn't exactly live outside you either. It hovers in a "nether space," not quite real, not quite fictitious. And yet at times it's bizarre enough to make a movie about.

For a long time, I didn't know what I had. I just thought that I was some raggedy bitch with a wildly unpredictable temper combined with equally unpredictable behavior, as in, you never knew which "me" you were going to get. And if I drank, it was worse.

On the other hand, people accepted this behavior because I was a phenomenal software developer, famous in the necessary circles for bleeding edge implementations. That means I wrote software for things only a few people had ever imagined.

Having already lead an interesting and frequently compelling life, and inspired to no small degree by the truly amazing and breath-taking Stanley Bert Eisen, I decided it would be a grand adventure to talk to some people who have only seen themselves through the eyes of strangers.

I started to do this and my friends started to say, *How can I help?* So here, We share what We know in Our songs, in Our lives, sometimes in the life-changing events that started... no, that sounds too easy: grabbed Us by somewhere and pulled Us off the path We were on and dropped Us on a new one. That's what happens and yes, it is certainly dramatic.

> This book is for those who can't yet speak for themselves. For those whose haunted eyes peer out at the world from within a protective shell.

PTSD and Me

You probably wonder *Who am I?* Mmmm. I used to wonder that a lot, too. I used to wonder why so many things about "Me" never seemed to mesh with things about "Them."

I'm not the only one who has been "brutally broken," to borrow from the gracious Keanu Reeves. There are thousands like Me, children who have grown up in the most unimaginable circumstances. Thousands, probably hundreds of thousands, who grow up without support, without boundaries, without safe places to be.

Happily, today I have boundaries; I have safe places to be; and, I share a wonderful, nurturing community with an extraordinary gang of people. Musicians all. And some amazing artists. Some who are both and some who are neither, happy instead to be just adoring fans.

My purpose in writing this book is to share with others – My Tribe of PTGers; others like Us who still grapple daily with the effects, triggers, behaviors; friends; significant others; parents; counselors; researchers; and, people who care and want to know: *What's it like to have PTSD? What is it like to live with the aftereffects of Trauma?* With its "comorbidities" like ADHD, OCD, and so on.

One thing that I noticed particularly while doing research for this book is that the Research Community has not focused very much on how touch tells feelings. But Musicians are all about touch. We care where Our fingers touch the fretboard, how they touch, how long the strings ring, how the movement from one note to another affects the rhythm. Drummers the same; horn players care about their hands, their fingers, and how their lips touch the mouthpiece. Every musician in the world cares about touch and cares about it in very great detail. And research has so often proven that music has the power to create deep and profound feelings that it now takes it as a given, and yet, it is treated as an external object, separate from the people making it. Interestingly, they treat PTSD & friends the same way, from the outside, a characteristic of the people who have it, but certainly not anything they would want to actually *engage* with.

Anything Else?

My World is small, my interests narrow, focused. But since you asked, there are two people I would really like to talk with. One of them is Paul Stanley; Stan Eisen, before he became Paul Stanley, The Starchild, is the person I would actually like to share with. His experience is similar to mine, but different. He had a traumatic childhood and so, like Me, doesn't have a "before. "But unlike Me, he still has that little gleam of pain in his eyes, so subtle you miss it – unless it is familiar because you have seen it in your own eyes, in the eyes of those you love. But the really beautiful thing about him is that "who he is" has always come out in his music. It's a particular kind of exquisite authenticity. The *I Was Made For Loving You* video is one of my favorites; *I Am Just A Boy* always teases tears.

For Me and for the people who have shared their stories, the lyrics to their songs of solace, wonder, hope, and yes, hurt, despair, the vehicle for connection is the music. With it, We have two things we are totally committed to: the Music and the challenges of Our daily lives. As Mr. Stanley says in Face the Music: "I was determined to survive."

Is there love after PTSD?

There must be because I'm as broken as anyone and yet I have the most amazing community of friends who love me, I don't know, because of me, in spite of me, because they see themselves in me, because I see myself in them. It's an amazing feeling.

And it's a totally amazing feeling to come out of what We call the darkness, see ourselves as broken AND lovable. To know that Our brokenness is not the prime contributor to why the people who We want to love can't communicate with Us, why they don't understand.

This book is first and foremost for Us, for those who have challenged PTSD and gotten a grip on its insidiousness.

It's also a book for those of Us who haven't gotten there yet (but will), who have been constrained in some way from sharing their experiences with others who understand. I hear every day, every heart-breaking day, about the loneliness that comes from the blank stares and the turning away by those who expect that Our stories should fit their experiences; that Our stories should all begin, *Once upon a time...*

Families, Friends & Significant Others

This book is for the people who have struggled to understand the challenges faced by their loved ones, challenges that are often so far beyond what families and friends expect from their ordinary experiences that they can't really imagine the reality of PTSD and its accompanying cognitive differences.

First Responders

It's for the people on the front lines, people in high-risk professions like first responders who must process their own reactions as well as those whom they are helping. Because here, too, it can be almost like a flashback scenario, where your Mind is processing two simultaneous and contradictory inputs.

Healthcare Professionals

Much of this will be new information for healthcare professionals, therapists, caregivers who can then take the first few little steps towards understanding across a huge chasm. This chasm is more dramatic I think than even all of PTSD itself. It is more dramatic, I think, because when We have PTSD, We already have all the "resources" to understand already in place. We already know what it feels like to have simultaneous, contradictory inputs. I know you can't imagine what it is *like*. People in general usually can't imagine what they haven't experienced in some way. In this book, I talk about how, exactly, that happens in a little dance among the Brain and its various inputs. And what happens to the Mind then. From the inside. From the place and time when my Mind has just taken a leave of absence. Or not. And I wish it would because it's not helping.

Researchers

And finally, this book is for researchers, who will hopefully see the error of their externally situated, statistics-laden ways and question who they are helping when they produce their frequencies and meta-analyses, those precious liners in their résumé path to tenure, to greater glory. This is how I see it right now, Folks, but like Us, you can change with the right understandings.

How to Use this Book

This book is for everyone who has been touched by PTSD in some way, maybe themselves, a friend, or a loved one.

Those who have experienced one or more traumatic events may find it helpful to be able to compare notes. I think this is especially important because my most fun times are those when I am hanging with my Tribe laughing delightedly over Our shared foibles: "You do that? I do that, too!" Peals of laughter ensue.

Veterans may find a distinct difference in frames of reference between the start of their traumatic events at age 18 and older, and mine at 18 months. I think most veterans have two frames of reference, the before and after. I'm not really sure. But I have only one; I have no before.

Mental health advocates may enjoy reading the comments and conversations because they provide an insight into a world essentially known by only those few – of the millions – who dare talk openly. There's a bit of a lingo; there's definitely what those who aren't Us would call Black Humor. And it is pretty dark, haunting. One of my friends commented: "They asked why. I told them it was how I survived."

About the Writing Style

The way I write is a Journey. If something is all one thought-stream, I show that to you as if it were music. I don't break it into smaller pieces because that's not the sound I hear in my head. I write what I hear, not what's conventionally expected.

Also, when I need a word that isn't already in the dictionary, I follow the time-honored tradition of making one up. For example, when did "googling" become a verb? It was the name of a company, didn't have "make it go" properties like a verb, and now, how many years later, it's a *verb*? So you may, scratch that, will, see things like "nuancy," which like all good adjectives simply means "having the properties of." I haven't decided if it should end in *cey* thus retaining its "nuance" properties strongly or without the *e*, where it just steps off on its own.

Research has not provided a specific term for the kind of "breaches of control" that We monitor and attempt to control, so in the time-honored tradition of new ideas everywhere, I created a word to say what I mean: Traumatic Break. This is different from The Trauma Event, or, simply, the Event. The "event," is what happened; the Traumatic Break is what We did in response.

I have formatted quotes two different ways depending on their source. If the words were spoken by someone, then they are placed in quotation marks. If they were text messages or communications with ChatGPT, them they are italicized. It seemed reasonable to distinguish between live context and digital context.

Songs in the Text

When I write, I often hear a song in my head. So I share that with you in in the text. And I write from the inside about situations We encounter, but I don't "clean it up." If I do, I will destroy the critical Connection inside. For example, here is a tiny example of a typical situation. This is a snarky question from someone trying to look smart: *How could you have PTSD if it wasn't diagnosed?*

Me: *oh, gee, maybe it was from those early skydiving lessons at 18-months; golly gee, maybe it was, hmm, maybe when "mom" only missed dad's heart by a quarter of an inch; maybe it was because I was so shell-shocked (old term, I know), anyway, I was so shell-shocked after 8 years of living in a war zone that I was unable to speak in any gathering greater than two, one of whom was me. Geez, maybe it was all that.*

[Pause]

Equally snarky: *I don't know; maybe it was all that. And more, what do you think?*

I have to admit I come at this with some inspiration from the very wonderful Paul Stanley. He's an inspiration because of his entire story. And because of his openness, authenticity, his willingness to talk. But what's sad is that there is still that little tinge of sadness in his eyes from "before."

My Clearest Hope For You

What I hope will be most useful for you is having found a place where you can say, Oh, yeah! That's me! And experience joy in saying it, because you can now see that "your Tribe" looks just like you. And that's a wondrous feeling. God bless!

Much love,

Aj Woernicki
San Miguel, NM, September 28, 2023

Embracing the Trauma Journey

> He played, and he sounded just like Bobby. He has Bobby's touch. And While my Mind was marveling, paying attention somewhere else, my Body "remembered" and Suddenly! I was back in New York City, back at the Lone Star, and Bobby was alive, and he was playing.
> And my Mind was screaming: No! Bobby's dead!
> And my ears were calmly, implacably saying, No, he's not. Listen!
> And my Mind split.
> And I went down hard and burned for a very long time.
> (C) 2024 AjWoernicki

My general way of being has been to walk away. To simply decide that caring wasn't something I was going to do any more. I wouldn't fight; I wouldn't argue. I would simply be gone.

Never to return.

I developed this paradigm when I was four years old. I had used it as an automatic stratagem, a conditioned behavior so familiar, so deeply embedded in my life, that I gave it little thought. I never questioned it in any way, especially never wondered if it was an appropriate way to be. It had protected me from hurt for a lifetime. There was little pain in turning away but the pain of wanting something I couldn't have was enormous. I think sometimes I am that tiny child again, reliving the string of canceled visits.

But this is a book of hope.

It is not a "horror story" book. It is honest, it is authentic, it is people in their own words. It is Our best effort to give you the best view we can of a room filled with smoke and mirrors.

Some of the stories make your heart clench, make your brain say that can't have happened, that can't be real. I assure you, it is real and for some of Us, many of Us, the challenges live and flourish every day. It is my deepest hope that others will find a common ground, a safe place to say, joyfully, "Oh, that's me," and through the Connections in this book, reflect with more gentleness and understanding upon the face of their own personal response to the simply unbelievable.

PTSD is a lot like a hurricane: Everyone sees the outside, the clouds, the wind, the rain...the damage...but only the Eye knows itself. And PTSD is like that. You seldom if ever hear people talk about what it's like, what it's really like. And I think We should; so I am.

Woven through the topics in this book is my story, what started it all, the Journey, where I am now. It's hard to write an authentic book about PTSD unless you have it; unless you live with it every day.

Strategies

I can't offer any strategies because there is simply no way for me to know what collection of "strategies," "tips," "tricks," might be effective for everyone who needs them. And it wouldn't be fair or truthful to suggest that I could.

So I share here what I did, what worked for me as spot-fixes, as long-term supports, and any pro's and con's I might have detected along the way. And others have shared what they did, what they are doing.

But truthfully, there is one and only one approach that has worked for all of us, and that's to take the time to really understand what We are dealing with. It's not the modern version of "Know Thyself;" it's seeing the elements of your response to trauma as outside yourself, "not-you," if you will.

My mother was not a nice person. I am imagining horrified responses: "But she was *Your Mother!*" "You shouldn't speak ill of the dead!" And so on. My mother was a truly horrible, mean individual who did everything she could to hurt me. She specialized in name-calling and was especially fond of critical adjectives.

When I was about 18, I applied for a job at the Friendlies restaurants in Boston. Part of the interview process was a psychological exam. In particular was a two-page form that had matching lists of words filling each physical page. On the left side, I was to circle all the words anyone had ever called me. On the right, I was to circle the words that described how I saw myself. I dutifully completed both pages.

Several days later, the HR director contacted me and apologizing profusely said that he had somehow mislaid my paperwork. Could I come down and redo it? I did.

Shortly after, we had another meeting and he held that two-page form in his hand. "How?" he said. "How is it that people have called you all these truly awful things and yet you still have a strong, positive view of yourself?"

I explained that my mother was a vicious, destructive person. I had realized that early on and simply didn't take anything she said to heart.

My home life took its toll, but at least I hadn't internalized the picture my mother painted of me.

Earlier this summer, I had intended to write the story of my childhood rather lightheartedly, since I think major parts of it are hysterically funny. But what happened was, in the way that's typical for songwriters, the heartbreaking true story of my parents flowed out onto the page. I was so raw, so painful, that I couldn't reread what I had written, couldn't share with others.

So while I describe my mother on somewhat less than glowing terms, I do realize there were reasons for why she was the way she was. I just don't care.

Can this book help you?

This is an authentic story that exposes the real inside of PTSD, written by the musicians and the artists who live It. And maybe in this way, We can help others to feel that they can be heard. And understood.

A note about terms: While "normal" and "crazy" seem to be an important distinction in everyday language, words that are flung about loosely to hurt, to injure, to joke, in serious conversation, mental health is very complex. This book addresses many of the subtle nuances of Our lives, of how We think and feel, what We do. I have made a distinction here, between Us, those who know what I am talking about on very deep levels, and Them, those who have no actual physical knowledge of what We manage every day. Sometimes, We experience great pain. As often, We experience great joy because what We have to do, what We have had to do to survive, has given us skills far beyond what others have. Our skills, what We can do, how We do it, is the result of hard work and determination.

In the way people usually talk, they use "Normal" to mean people who act and think in ways that seem to be the same as what everyone else in their social context does. It is supposed to mean that what people do, how they feel, and what they think are similar to what others around them think and feel.

Here is an example from one of my favorite authors, L.T. Ryan. In Deep State: A Bear Logan Thriller, the characters are facing a challenging operation. Sadie and Bear are seasoned operatives while Cara is an investigative reporter. Watch what happens to Cara's choice of language.

> *Sadie grabbed a folder from the table and handed it to Bear. "Nothing good. These guys are the best. And I mean that literally. I've never seen a track record as good as this. They work as a pair, so there's always a contingency plan. They don't miss, Bear. Not ever." "We've had worse odds before." "I haven't." Cara's voice was quiet. "This is insane. You know that, right?"*

In this situation, Cara does not have enough experience to understand how everything will work out. And so she expresses this by using a culturally- common term. She says, This is insane. And then, she says, *You know that, right?* looking for confirmation, a frightened disbelief that Bear and Sadie might not be in agreement with what is so obvious to her.

"Crazy" -or "insane" – are terms often used to disparage or demean people who are different, people who think or feel differently from what is considered "the norm." You will frequently hear people say, Oh that's so crazy. Or Alice Cooper is so crazy; KISS is so crazy.

In cities and towns across the country, people who have lost touch with reality in the clinical sense share the streets with those who have become homeless because of financial reasons. We see them walking the roads chatting with friends only they know or see. And We are afraid. We are afraid for the simple reason that We cannot communicate with these people. We feel that We could be in danger because they wouldn't understand Our words, Our feelings. We don't understand who they are, why they are here, living on the street. And because We are afraid, We create and use a "push-away" term. We call them "crazy." It's intended to distinguish "Them" from "Us."

Mental challenges – as a crazy person myself, I refuse to use the popular term mental *illness*. This makes it sound like there is no way out; or like only medication in the form of pills or shots can cure the *problem*, the *affliction*. I know that is not true because I have lived it. Others have lived it, are living it.

Nothing We have experienced ever really goes away. It is imprinted on us forever, sometimes in subtle ways, sometimes more dramatically. So PTSD never really "goes away" but We can not only learn to live with it fairly successfully, We can also learn to enjoy the special skills and insights it gives us. And some of this, just a little bit considering the broad sweep of Our amazing lives, is what you will find yourself sharing in these pages. You will see a little bit of the enormous creativity that emerges when the brain is allowed to travel down different pathways. So when you see the amazing things We have done, that other musicians and artists have done, don't think "I can't do that. That's crazy." Think, "Wow. Look at what those people can do because their lives have been different in a lot of ways." Think: "those people rock."

Why is this book unique?

What is incredibly unique about this book, about these stories, is that every single person, each glorious individual, has slogged their way through their own personal 'whatever' to achieve a new level of their own kind of comfort. Is 'It' all gone? Oh hell no. But everyone has the joy and pleasure of having gotten one over on this "Thing" that most people only know how to reference from a far distance.

This book is unique in that it's told almost entirely by those who have PTSD. We talk openly about what it's like to be triggered. We share how it feels to deal with the responses to the triggered behaviors. And, as a Tribe, We share what We have done to manage Our lives in a world often without help and without hope. This, for the first time ever in print, is Our story.

Why is PTSD different?

PTSD is different from other mental challenges because memories of the trauma, sometimes memories only related to the initial trauma come back. Again. And again.

And sometimes they come back very fast, and you are living in two worlds. In the one that has taken over your consciousness, you are back in a time and place that has meaning to you. But in the other world, the one where you are right now, your body is still taking inputs, and feeding them to all the usual places.

What's It Like?

What's it like to have PTSD. I mean, what's it LIKE, really LIKE? What does it feel like in your body? What does it feel like when something has a grip inside you and you are being carried along by something you don't recognize and you can't stop? When you feel like you are just an observer?

What does it feel like to come out of a blackout triggered by rage triggered by a physical response to a 'situation?' To wonder where you are? What you did? How much it's going to take to clean up the mess… what does it feel like? We tell you what some of that is for us.

Posttraumatic Growth

Most people don't know that the fun, bright side to PTSD is called "Posttraumatic Growth." In this book, We share Our gains and Our joys, and how We got there. We have all worked very hard to show you a view, a view carefully crafted in human terms, that is, through the words, the eyes, the ears, lives, of the people who actually have it. Maybe more what Our Bodies have done than what Our pesky Minds brought to the fray.

A Note on the Research

You will not find a list of "symptoms" abstracted by the analytical community, people on the outside trying to look in. This book will not rely too much on the published academic research because of its heavy reliance on gathering information on various "characteristics" that are then fed through sophisticated statistical analyses to produce reports that say, Oh look, we've shown "whatever" and this is "bad." We need more "next whatever." Solutions are offered infrequently. This makes sense because researchers are looking from the outside in.

My Goals

But really what I want to do in this book is to tell you what it's like: How does it feel to have PTSD? When I look at what's been published, there are no books like this, written by a survivor, helped by others, other musicians and artists, who have firsthand experience.

The voices of the people who actually have "it" have been relegated to clinical treatment settings, shrouded in secrecy and shame. Where, you know, it's like: Oh my God you can't tell. And then it's like: Yes I can sweetheart, oh for God's sakes, yeah I can!"

What does it take to get there? First of all, it takes nerve. I mean, people talk about bravery and courage as if it were some part of a story and you know, it is some part of a story. It's a story of the never-ending hero.

I wish all of you all the best on the big Journey that is your life, and in the little journeys that make up your days and nights, your hopes and fears, your dreams and failures. Because it really is all a mixed bag, you know.

Why do you want to read this book?

#1 Reason: The book is dope!

#2 Reason: See Reason #1.

1: Trauma's Mind Effects

We live in a world battered by the incessant emails of AI-fueled marketing strategies; the sounds of war here and around the world; the sounds of traffic, children screaming, children shooting, children dying.

We live in a world where veterans of endless wars cope with the unseen attacks on their centers of stability by the unseen, often unconsidered sounds of war.

We live in a world where people still shelter from "The Covid." A world where the unseen influences of a world under siege battered the psyches of billions. Millions died; many more have "Long Covid."

The impact that the COVID-19 pandemic has had on the number of PTSD cases worldwide in now being recognized for the enormity that it is. Previously, PTSD, like pretty much all other cerebral challenges, was a dirty little secret that happened to "them," "over there," not "us," "over here."

This fear, this terrible fear of you looking at me like I was a monster...

My makeup was a mask that provided distance between me and the crowd. It gave me the shield I needed. (Stanley, 2014)

With COVID, the chances that PTSD, depression, melancholia, and related miseries are now living with you in your home are very high. That they are impacting people you work with, worship with, shop, play and relax with, are 100%. This unbelievable number is due to the incredible stresses along so many dimensions that COVID rained down, not upon specific populations or specific places, but on the whole world all at the same time.

And people need help. They need to understand. They need to change how they see the "dirty little secret" because it is no longer relegated to "them," "over there," because "They" became "Us" in the hot Covidic crucible, and simultaneously, "There" became "Here."

But more than getting sick, people lived with the possibilities of becoming sick, of possibly dying. It was day to day watching the numbers of cases, of deaths, spread across the world. Spread to families, to friends in distant lands, heard the church bells calling out, saw the bodies piled in refrigerator trucks, unable to be cared for in the onslaught of death and trauma.

Underneath all the activity outside was the psychological impact inside, for some, the psychological devastation of the long spells of quarantine.

Most startling for me is the reflection of "the Cascade" of Events in the research. In healthcare settings, many frontline workers faced overwhelming workloads, life-and-death decisions, patient mortality, worries about infecting family or loved ones, and other traumas, leading to a cascade of mental health problems, one following after another, each contributing to the others until they became indistinguishable.

According to a review published in the Journal of Anxiety Disorders, up to a quarter of healthcare workers in intensive care units met the criteria for PTSD during the pandemic, reflecting similar statistics seen in populations who had experienced disaster or combat situations.

Reports from Italian investigators found that 30% of COVID-19 survivors who had had severe infections still suffered from PTSD a month after their hospital treatment. (Janiri, 2021)

The pandemic has also seen an increase in what's known as "vicarious traumatization" among the general public — trauma that results from being repeatedly exposed to graphic details of traumatic events.

And because of the ongoing stress caused by the Pandemic that doesn't really seem to go away, We are just at the beginning of trying to understand the impact that this event may have on people when, instead of living in a world of "normals" with a few crazies, they are now living in a world of "crazies" with a few "normals."

Ordinary people see "normal" as whatever is usual and customary within their particular world structure, whether it be composed solely of family and a few friends or extend more widely, including particular interest groups and activities.

Statistically, "normal" can be defined by the researcher but is generally considered to be within two standard deviations from the mean. The mean is simply the average of all the values. They add up all the values and divide by how many there are.

This image shows the different shapes of bell curves that occur in data streams of all kinds. And, actually, in research, the values outside the "normal" range excite the most interest.

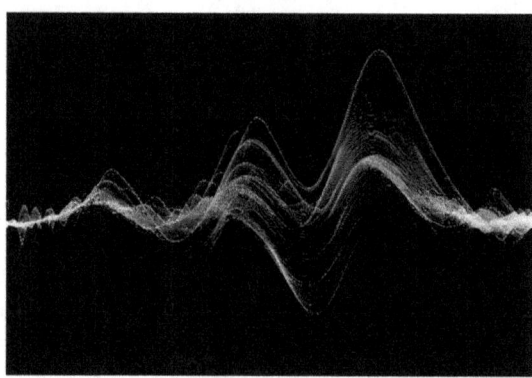

How does Research See PTSD?

Besides what I see, there is another "world view," a weltanschauung in German, and it is the world view held by the research community. From their work have come many dull, dry, outside-in and "abstracted for objectivity" lists. Lists of what plagues us in *The Literature*.

But here is my version: The Research labels are bolded.

Emotional instability. What's really important to think about here is what kinds of behaviors constitute "Emotional stability." The research generalizations are "Rapid mood changes," (this was my dad).

Frequent Sadness. In addition, some people have anxiety, some report depression. But I am not sure where the number is that separates the "frequencies." Is it five times a day? Five times a week? A month? Is Five not a good number? And why are the people sad? Is it related to the series of trauma events? Or is there some other reason? One weakness with academic research is that people often structure questions so the results support what they believe to be true.

Recollection of Past Trauma. These come as flashbacks, nightmares, both, or some weird combination of "two places," being in the here and now and being in "that other place" at the same time. These experiences don't need to be about a specific event, but will relate to it in some way. One weakness here is that the research doesn't seem to have recognized the speed factor in how fast a Trigger can produce a behavior.

Difficulty with Relationships. From my point of view, this is absolutely true and it is directly related to what the person you are trying to connect with knows about who you are. Some people view us as just "normal people who have anger management issues." This is obviously simplistic and leads to communication misfires. On the other hand, I find it much easier to connect with people who have had to overcome challenges in their lives. I find it especially easy to connect with people who are struggling with my kind of "crazy." They are usually a really good hang.

Self-blame or guilt. Personally, I only felt guilty about one thing, and that is the poor raccoon I ran over in the dark one night in New Hampshire. I miscalculated our mutual speeds. I still think that if I had erred on the side of caution, slowed down just to be on the safe side, that raccoon would have lived out a normal life. But then, recently, with new realizations has come new guilt, a wishing that I had been a better person. This is only indirectly related to my early childhood events.

Avoidance of Triggers. We can try to avoid things, people, sounds, smells, hopes, dreams, and fears that might remind Us of what happened, what continues to happen in the cinematography in our Brains. Sometimes, one of what I call "hairTriggers," gets you unawares.

The medical community has specific definitions for various illnesses and conditions. The Diagnostic and Statistical Manual of Mental Disorders is the resource that therapists, psychiatrists, and other medical personnel use to determine diagnoses. The Third Edition was published in 1980; the Fourth in 1994; and, the Fifth Edition in 2013; The most recent edition is DSM-5-TR published in 2022. The big change was the addition of "prolonged grief disorder."

What Is Trauma?

Simply put, *Trauma* is when really bad stuff happens to you.
Especially stuff nobody believes you about.

But in the 1980 publication of the Diagnostic and Statistical Manual of Mental Disorders, more commonly known as the DSM-III, when PTSD was first added, it had a very tight criterion. It was what they called a "'monocausal' mental disorder." This single cause had to be "significant," and "Generally outside the range of usual human experience." This sadly means that you won't be able to explain it to anyone because people can't really understand things they haven't experienced, except abstractly, like learning from a textbook. If I say, "I fell down and skinned my knee," most people have one or several memories they can call up, relive, sometimes even feel the pain of the cut. If I say, "I didn't sleep for two years," people can't really understand what this feels like. And really, it's all about being able to feel what something is like, to feel it in our arms and legs, our bodies, in musicians' cases, in our fingers, lips, ears, eyes, and in the synaesthetic creation that is our expression of the understanding that emerges from that experience. A lot of us have synaesthesia, where inputs from one sense translate also into outputs from another. When I hear individual notes, I "see" them in color; harmonics are multi-colored cascades, not unlike the image above.

Where I Stand

There's a lot to "talking about Trauma." First, there's the *Assault* itself. This takes many forms and has impacts and implications along many dimensions. Second, there are the *Effects* of the assault on the soul, body and mind; and, finally, there is the *Denial* from the unbelieving. For musicians, that's an A major chord: A, E, D. 1, 4, 5. And the 5 is a wrap. Not being believed is the worst of all.

Understanding the Words

Words seem simple but they are really very complicated.

Most people see events as *bundles.* They don't see them as a series of discrete actions. Further, they are elaborated – that means creating an interesting story of what happened, stuff based on usually what your (probably yappy) Mind is saying. This "interesting story" now has blended all the precise details into a single event, regardless. And this, in the DSM, is what is called *monocausal* – a single action is the cause of what happened.

The Child fell down and cried. This is an event in its simplest actions. It seems simple enough, and for most people, until now, it is enough. But We are talking about trauma here, so let's shift into an equally authentic worldview: *The Child fell down and didn't cry.* Most people would be grateful because they wouldn't have to cope with clean-up, with comforting the child. They could go on with their lives as before, the unfortunate event just a tiny blip in their day.

But before we leave, How did the child fall down. Did she trip on a broken walkway? Over something that shouldn't have been there? Was she pushed? And by whom? Was he being bullied? So many questions that can *lead* to the presumed single cause of the crying, that the child cried just because, only because, he or she *fell down*.

But again, all we know from the statement is that the child is crying. We don't know whether physical or emotional responses are facilitating the crying. Is the child's knee hurting? Does the child feel guilty about tearing their good pants? Better yet, is the child rehearsing for a play?

It seems so many questions can arise from very simple statements. Even simple phrases or words. I was reading Deep State: A Bear Logan Thriller. It's by L. T. Ryan. Bear and best friend Jack were discussing the next mission and Jack says, "Imagine something like the Treaty of Versailles for the countries of the Middle East..."

The book continues on the assumption that readers know about the broader implications of the Treaty: that is, that they know why such a suggestion would be a serious threat also in the Middle East. Most readers would brush right past, believing that the author will tell them more if they need to know.

Here's where a seemingly unrelated even in popular culture relates closely to how people understand and relate to PTSD and mental challenges in general.

How Deep Are the Questions?

I recalled "the Treaty of Versailles" but I had never really considered the "broader impacts." This is a phrase we will see also in discussions about research.

So I went to ChatGPT and typed in the following request:

> hello. What do you know about the Treaty of Versailles. Include if you can the geopolitical and economic impacts and outcomes, if you distinguish

ChatGPT responded with:

> The Treaty of Versailles was a peace treaty signed on June 28, 1919, that officially ended World War I. It was signed between Germany and

> the victorious Allied powers, including France, the United Kingdom, Italy, and the United States.
>
> Geopolitically, the treaty had significant consequences. Germany was held responsible for the war and was forced to accept full blame, which led to territorial losses. The treaty redrew the map of Europe, resulting in the disintegration of the German Empire <u>and the creation of new countries such as Poland, Czechoslovakia, and Yugoslavia.</u>
>
> The harsh economic burden placed on Germany also fueled resentment and anger, setting the stage for future political tensions and ultimately played a role in the rise of Adolf Hitler and the Nazis.

What surprised me most was the suggestion that Poland was created as a "new country," along with Yugoslavia and Czechoslovakia. So I asked Google, *What year did Poland become a country?*

From Poland – Countries – Office of the Historian

> Poland vanished from the map of Europe until 1918; Napoleon created a Grand Duchy of Warsaw from Prussian Poland in 1807, but it did not survive his defeat.
>
> [Aj: A country "vanished?" Vanished?]
>
> A Polish Republic was proclaimed on November 3, 1918. On November 14, General Joseph Pilsudski became head of state. <u>On January 17, 1919, a cabinet was formed with pianist Ignace Jan Paderewski as its Prime Minister. (Jasiewicz et al., 2024)</u>

Of course it was. And of course he was. Poland is famous for its pianists: Chopin, born in 1810; Arthur Rubinstein, born in 1887; Contemporary pianist Krystian Zimerman, born in 1956; and, of course, Paderewski, who died in 1941.

But, to return to 'A country "vanished?"' How does a country vanish?

So one more question, to Google: When was Poland at the height of its power?

Britannica helped out with this:

> In the mid-1500s, united Poland was the largest state in Europe and perhaps the continent's most powerful nation.
>
> Yet two and a half centuries later, during the Partitions of Poland (1772–1918), it disappeared, parceled out among the contending empires of Russia, Prussia, and Austria.

This discussion was a bit of an excursion into my personal history: nowhere in the oral history of my family from the "disputed" area can I recall stories about a "vanishing." I do remember "the Old Country" being more a "flavor of the day." The farms always remained the same, like the song, but the names of the tunes and the labels who owned them changed daily, sometimes hourly. I was born here, but along with not having a *Before* history, I don't really have a place history for the grandparents who provided me safe haven in my early, vulnerable years.

So now that we know that grandma and hence me, too, are from "disputed Eastern Europe" we can get on with why these seemingly disconnected stories are very relevant to PTSD and to different methods of PTSD research.

When someone reads a reference as in "the Treaty of Versailles," they may or may not stop to ask the next set of questions: What is the author telling us about the plot? About the underlying geopolitics and economics?

When people ignore data that seems in the way because they don't understand it, they end up being oblivious to substantial portions of the story. In this case, learning that the social response to the harshness of the Treaty lead to the rise of Hitler may be important in the story. It certainly was to the world, to the soldiers, and to the six million Jews who died leaving endless families without a context.

The truths of traumas of Auschwitz-Birkenau, of Bergen-Belsen, Treblinka, Dachau will break a Mind that tries to understand.

Perhaps this potential "breakage" is what characterizes certain types of PTSD research, particularly in the psychological domains. The hurt buried beneath the surface is indeed beyond human experience.

Changing Medical Definitions

The limited scope of the DSM description brought a lot of criticism from a lot of doctors, therapists, researchers in the field, other interested parties. They wrote papers that included suggestions, criticisms, and some outright rubbish about raising ordinary stress to a medical condition. How one gets from "outside the range of usual human experience" to "ordinary stress" is a marvel of academic ad hominem attacks.

However, when the DSM-5 was published in 2013, the definition had both softened and expanded:

A. Exposure to actual or threatened death, serious injury, or sexual violence in one (or more) of the following ways:
   1. Directly experiencing the traumatic event(s).
   2. Witnessing, in person, the event(s) as it occurred to others.
   3. Learning that the traumatic event(s) occurred to a close family member or close friend. In cases of actual or threatened death of a family member or friend, the event(s) must have been violent or accidental.
   4. Experiencing repeated or extreme exposure to aversive details of the traumatic event(s) (e.g., first responders collecting human remains; police officers repeatedly exposed to details of child abuse). (p. 271)

Also under fire was the constraint, *monocausal*. This is just like it sounds: one thing – "mono" – is responsible for what happened – "causal," the cause. Example: my mother tossed me headfirst out the window. This was the single cause of my landing on the concrete below. It was not the cause of my landing on my head. That was due to other factors. But it was partially the cause of my resultant head trauma, and so on. It was what we could call "a precipitating event."

But the concept of "monocausal" doesn't really address the complexity of mental challenges such as PTSD. Further, PTSD becomes a self-fulfilling prophecy: from the initial trauma arise feelings of pain fear, loss, later confusion, separation. The duration of a break can vary widely depending on the speed of the physical response to the stressor. More on this later, because it's really interesting how it happens.

What Do People Talk About?

First, there's *Acute Trauma*. This usually is what happens to your Brain, to your Body, to your Mind, from just one Event. The Event can be dangerous, like being shot at or defending yourself or someone else, or it can be really stressful, like watching someone die.

Next there's *Chronic Trauma*. This is when the Bad Stuff keeps happening over and over. For me, it was living in the war zone that masqueraded as "My Home." Other examples are daily abuse to children whose tiny, new minds fracture at the dystopia. This is when their physical inputs are contradicting the knowledge in their genes. Domestic Violence, always a problem, has increased enormously during COVID, interacting with the other Stressors. And of course, there's War.

Complex Trauma is my personal favorite because it is so easy to describe as *Totally Fucked*, occasionally referred to as *TF*. It can also be described as "the gift that keeps on giving." This is the kind of trauma response that intrudes on your personal spaces, over and over. And it usually comes in multiple kinds. A web search concludes that this "occurs repeatedly and cumulatively, usually over a period of time and within specific relationships and contexts." What this "objective assessment" doesn't tell you is that these "specific relationships" and other groups, social situations, and so on are kept in place more often than not for basic survival needs. It's a Catch-22 for the person. Researchers don't get this because they are looking only along a single dimension. By the way, trying to force-match what you are observing to the view in your head, no matter who does it, is a Power & Control issue.

Secondary Trauma: This is sometimes called "vicarious" because it is "living through the experiences of someone else." Ordinary people often don't realize that listening to the descriptions of the traumatic experiences of others can be very painful, and can create emotional duress. And this affects the very people whose job it is to respond in traumatic situations, dangerous situations; to be there listening, helping, comforting, in times of great trouble. As violence increases across the world, and as pandemics such as COVID become possible under the relentless destruction of the Environment that keeps us well, doctors, emergency responders, psychologists, and people who work with children and animals, victims who often cannot speak for themselves, are especially vulnerable.

Developmental or Childhood Trauma occurs when a child lives in a place with people who make his or her lives terrible by abusing them in the many unbelievable ways parents, other family, friends and caregivers have of torturing and terrorizing helpless children.

Put more abstractly, less viscerally, a web search described it as "where a child experiences or witnesses chronic interpersonal trauma early in life, such as physical or sexual abuse." If we expand the possibilities, this means that some children experience every possible kind of the types of traumas described above. I find that to be an absolutely horrifying thought. Even though I lived through a cascade just like that.

What's Different Here?

The previous five items are the names for the different ways traumas are characterized *in the academic literature*. This means that when people are doing research, and publishing books and papers, these are the common ways they will use to reference specific types of what I like to think of as the Event Horizons. The song here would be the Eagles "Hotel California: You can check in but you can never check out."

PTSD is a lot like a hurricane

Post-Traumatic Stress Disorder (PTSD) is what happens to *You*: to your Body, to your Brain, to your Mind, your Heart: to everywhere you know, after the *Bad Thangs* happen. It's what happens when your Mind tries to "make meaning," to make sense of what your Body is saying on one level and what your Brain is saying on another. Your Mind will try to make sense of the conflicting inputs, and if it tries hard enough and doesn't succeed, it crashes and burns. In a later chapter here is the story of the time that my Mind did. And I tell you how and why, every little piece.

DSM Advances

Over time, a biopsychosocial model reflected a more enlightened view, taking into account the different factors – and combinations of those factors – that contribute to the different behaviors based on how Our minds *now* work.

It is important to note here, at least as I see it, that We will never be the same as We were before. One main factor contributing to this irreversibility is that We know more. PTSD and its related "comorbidities," that is, the "bad stuff that goes along with," like Borderline Personality Disorder, force Us to think about different things. These include things that We never considered before, and also, how We might make sense of the strange and often unpleasant things Our Brains seem to be doing. The DSM says these "strange and often unpleasant things" can include:

> *re-experiencing the traumatic event; numbing of responsiveness to, or reduced involvement with, the external world; and a variety of autonomic, dysphoric, or cognitive symptoms. [DSM-III, p. 236]*

Autonomic symptoms

Research has tended to investigate each of a collection of observable, reproducible "symptoms." Generally, a research project will focus on a single "symptom" and report low-hanging results: Seligowski, et al. looked at women with PTSD, with or without dissociation. What they reported was what's known as "standard frequencies: race, age, level of education, and the percentages of different types of traumatic event(s). A requirement of research is that there be some benefit to the people who share their bodies and minds for research. One must ask how a table of externally observable characteristics benefits anyone except the people who now have a nice liner on their résumés.

D'Andrea, et al. reported that "participants with severe, prolonged trauma exposure and severe symptoms will experience blunted autonomic reactivity, while participants with more attenuated exposure and symptoms will experience elevated autonomic reactivity." Both of these sets of results were determined by measuring physical responses such as heart beats and breaths, skin temperature and wetness. An unobvious weakness in these and similar research designs is that they use consistent, structured stimuli – loud sounds, basically – to create the traumatic response.

The "exaggerated startle" is a popular research topic; however, there is no proof that the "research population," the participants, i.e., the people participating in the research, has the trauma-induced brain configuration that will produce the desired result under the Predicting condition. I have a startle response to loud noises, and under the right emotional circumstances, I will totally remove myself from a situation, even if my body is still there. It's a form of dissociation, it seems. I am never sure when people say "dissociation" if they mean the really extreme end where people lose all touch with reality, or if they mean the more practical approach many of Us use to isolate from hurtful situations. I learned this technique about the time I was four and a half.

Dysphoric Symptoms

The word dysphoria comes from two ancient Greek words that mean "bad to bear." Another possible wording is "difficult to bear." I chose the former because it is closer to the physical feeling, to what the Body is realizing. "Difficult" is more what the Mind would think, comparing this particular event to others that might be more or less "difficult" things.

"Bad," on the other hand, has more immediacy, and tends to imply, if not invoke, an immediate *physical* reaction, pulling away by some action.

From my perspective – and this could be only mine – if I can say, "Sheesh, that was *difficult,* it means I am in enough control that my pesky Mind is having its minute in the sun, and I look pretty "normal" to Them. If something is "bad," I'm never going to make it to "difficult:" my Body is going to have reacted in some way to insure my survival, however it interprets that.

Dysphoria shows itself in different ways. Some people are always negative, have a hard time finding the happy or funny side of anything. For some there is chronic irritability, a persistent agitation that feels like a constant need to go somewhere, to do something. Some people have difficulty concentrating, and others cope with a wide range of sleep disturbances, including vicious, repetitive nightmares.

The Biopsychosocial Model

With more research, and the discussions, arguments, and popular ad hominem attacks that characterize Research activities in general, there has emerged a more fully aware model of PTSD. This is called the Biopsychosocial Model. It is called that because it is 3-dimensional in its view of what and how PTSD is. It is far more comprehensive and *realistic* than previous views because it recognizes that like all health, and in fact all life, exists in the complex interplay of biological, psychological, and social factors.

The Biological dimension looks at a person's physical health. This includes genetics, because there is some indication that some people are more likely to have PTSD because of their genetic makeup. Similarly, some people might have a natural immunity for the same or different genetic factors.

Particularly with PTSD, the biochemical responses are critical components. We all talk about those responses that are slow enough that we can trap them and control them cognitively. And then there are others that occur at the speed of light, much faster than we can handle.

A third consideration is whether there was some pre-existing disease, or whether the person was hurt at the same time.

The psychological aspects account for much of the control that We have acquired. How We get on depends a great deal on what We think, what We believe, and especially, how We tell Our stories.

If We believe We are victims, We are. If We are helpless and pitiful in the ways We tell Our stories, We are. Everyone in this book has struggled with images of who they are, who they want to be. Some of Us still do. Some of Us have terrible, almost debilitating anxiety about getting up on that stage. But We do it anyway because that's Who We Are.

Stories and Our Social Circles

I think that the most important aspect of managing how Our bodies react in Our lives is how We create the social circles where We can tell Our stories as We see them. Our natural, healing humor is dark, black, filled with busses, knives, bombs, told with peals of laughter and exclamations of "Me, too!" "Me, too." New research on the effects of the Ukrainian war is showing that living with a friend is a significant factor in mitigating the potential for PTSD and c-PTSD (Velykodna, et al., 2024). In other words, sharing with a friend can keep you healthy.

To be with others who know, where You don't have to try to explain, is relaxing and fun. But We all have different coping strategies. Some people I know are working on trying to be okay within their pre-existing social groups, especially family. Others, like Me, opt for a clean break away from problematic behaviors and attitudes. My siblings were drug dealers. Not the life I wanted.

Each of Us tests the different situations, checks to see how We are doing, prepares for disaster clean-up. Always. There's no way We can avoid every Trigger, every smell, sound, touch, memory that can take Us back in less than the blink of an eye. We have to learn to accept that sometimes, something unpredictable, something unexpected is going to happen and We are going to have a melt-down of some sort. Ooops!

One of the attitudes that I have learned personally is that things are going to happen, and if I stress over them after the fact, I will usually make things worse. So I let a lot of things go.

2: Hello, Trauma. You're Me.

For those whose haunted eyes peer out at the world from within a protective shell.

Everything and nothing about PTSD is funny. But everything and nothing is especially not funny when no one but Us knows that there is a very big difference between when trauma occurs so early in life that you are not aware, that there is another way to be; and, that everyone is not like you.

It takes a while to realize why They just don't get it. And the length of that "while" is exactly equal to the length of time it takes to meet that first person in your life who listens to you and says, "Yeah. Me, too!"

A lot of Us here sharing Our stories built from the Music that sustains Us have no "Before." We have only life with PTSD. We know of nothing *Before*, no mores, no social acculturation, no sense of how it feels to feel comfortable in a crowd. We have none of that. We have made it to these pages because We have two things: An almost total ignorance of how being any other way would be; and two, an almost joyful passion of trying to beat the pesky intrusion at its own game.

> the children we meet in our practices often come to us having internalized society's message of denial. Their demoralization and disbelief in the possibility of change often is rooted in the fact that their disclosures were not believed
>
> (Silberg, 2022)

We don't always talk much, depending on the complex ambience, but those of Us who are close always keep a gentle physical connection with Our bodies. It's tough to explain how this works. My Mind isn't "doing" this; my Body is. I don't have to Think about it, hence involving the Mind, because my Body has already assessed any action-level potential. If my Body is uncomfortable, time to engage the Brain for a discussion. Mind stays quiet because this is serious and its yappy opinion will only kludge things up. (Like playing; We can't let it talk then either.)

My First Skydiving Practice

It's a beautiful day. In the neighborhood. The sky is blue, maybe a few clouds. Fruit trees are in bloom, bees flitting from blossom to blossom. The grass is green, still damp with early dew. Birds sing happily, building nests with their mates. Daffodils and crocuses dance in the gentle breeze.

Overhead, a tiny blonde child slides down the slate of the grand Victorian house, leaving a blood streak as she passes. Eyes wide, she thinks: *How do I do this? This is gonna hurt.*

Over the edge now, she delights in the freefall, thinking nothing more than, *Ooooo, this is fun.* And then, Smack! Followed by Plop! As her body – my Body – hits the ground. *Ooops! Yup! That hurt.*

The neighbor lady comes out, sees that the expected doll in her mind is not matching the silent object on the ground, and chaos ensues.

Are You OK? No, but I'm Funny

What was I thinking as I flew out that window. We know I wasn't immediately in free fall because I scraped my face on the slate. Apparently, the healing of that mess was nothing short of miraculous.

But here I am. "Somehow" I have navigated my way up the 3 feet to the open(?), open really? window and crawled through. You know, maybe the window was all the way up and I was walking on the sill. My family never said anything about that but, you know. Strange things happen.

So here I am, however I got here. I'm sliding down the slate. How fast? How wide is the roof? Has to be two and a half feet. Or so. So I slide. Slowly. Down the roof. Face first. Well, just one side. There's a tiny scar still left.

Think Anime eyes. What am I thinking. Has my sense of the Absurd kicked in? In that case, Ooops. This is gonna maybe hurt?

Am I scared? Apparently not because I wasn't crying. My rescuer – just for that Event – would have heard. But there was no sound. She had to look to see it was me and not the presumed doll.

Here's where It gets interesting. Calculating free fall at 20 feet and Earth gravity at 32 feet every second squared, my fall, not counting the slide down the roof, took 1.115 seconds. Now, here's the rub: was I really smart before the fall? Or just after? I'm gonna go with before, because you know, you have to be really miserable to throw your kid out the window.

So, here we are, smart kid on the adventure of her young – and so far, only moderately troubled life – and now she's flyyyy-ing! How many people wish they could fly. Here I was. Flying high above the ground, time seemingly endless, soft blonde curls flying in the increasing wind speed. We all know about increasing wind speed in New Mexico.

And Then What Happened?

This was the first of a succession of theoretically traumatic events. My dad took me to live with my maternal grandparents because he feared for my safety, for my life.

Neither of them visited very often, but my dad was the only one who came to see me. And that was rarely and always at the end of a string of broken promises, strings of dreamt-of visits that never happened. And somewhere between the now very wise ages of four and four and a half, I decided that hoping people who never came would come was not fun. So I decided to stop doing it. And my parents became incidental, unimportant in my life. I simply stopped caring if they came or not.

And What Happened Next?

I always wanted to be something different. There always seemed to be something better just on the, just on the other side of this, this wall with, this wall was transparent and gray and kind of ombre, darker on the bottom and lighter on the – no darker on the top and lighter on the bottom. But this other thing, it was a thing, not a possibility like I might think of it now, but no, it was a thing. It was, it was better, it was me but better and I couldn't get there.

And that's how it was for a long, long time.

And then when I was eight, my Grandpa died. And the real hell began. I was sedated for three days because my mother couldn't deal with a crying child who had just lost the person closest to her. Six months later, my Grandma broke her wrist and couldn't care for me. My Dad carried me, kicking and screaming, to the house already filled with the aforementioned mother, and two siblings, a boy and a girl, whom I didn't really know. Having had entire rooms to myself for most of my life, having to share the second floor with two other people – and it wasn't that big – was really bad news.

And Then It Began to Rain Down Hell

Three weeks later, there is a war zone. And it's loud and it's underneath us. Brother and sister are crying; I'm aggravated. I creep down the stairs, open the door at the bottom, and look around the corner, through the small dining room to the kitchen beyond.

My father, on my right, is holding a percolator full of hot coffee. My mother, on my left, is holding a 12-inch slicing knife. My Mind imagines the worst happening. I faint in the hallway.

The wars continue; somehow I graduate. But before I do, my nine-year-old projection becomes a fully-fledged reality as my mother actually puts that knife through my father's chest, missing his heart by a literal millimeter. Not for trying, I'm sure.

Dad finally moves out and I'm almost outta there myself. But in the meanwhile, I've started smoking; drinking; and, I've wrecked my mother's car drag racing with my boyfriend. Even then I was living on the Edge.

Having lived in terror for so many years, having been where the terror rolled like lava into Our unprotected world, I was already an adrenaline junkie, always on the prowl for the next high. I found my thrill, not on Blueberry Hill, but in software development. It was the Wild West. I loved it.

So What's It Like Now?

Now is very much what we are talking about. After years of confusion, of sensing that I didn't fit in, of not knowing why, *now* is a very happy place. The drinking, suicide attempts, the car wrecks, are all relics of the past.

Getting here wasn't easy. But more than that, PTSD seems to be something people don't recognize unless it's in a clinical setting or unless it's expected. People don't talk about it; it's stigmatized. I don't know if life would have been better if I'd known what it was earlier. Drugs, alcohol, music, and successful software implementations kept me flying high for a very long time. And then, at the height of my career, I met Bobby, and things changed. He loved me, and I don't think I knew what love was, but I gave him everything I could. And then the PTSD reared its ugly head; my fear of what I didn't know rushed all over me and I was a train wreck. And he still loved me, that wonderful man.

And What's It Really Like Now?

We are talking about what it's like to still have PTSD but be more in control: from the inside out, as musicians. This is something most people have never seen and I am absolutely in love with the opportunity to share.

The people who have shared their thoughts and their work are my friends. It's nice to have friends. But not just *any* friends: my friends all share three characteristics: They are all creative; they have all been impacted by traumatic events; and, they all push through it, sometimes daily, sometimes minute by minute. This pushing through, developing new skills, understanding Our Minds better, this is Posttraumatic Growth. And it's magnificent.

3: We Were Only Children

PTSD: That's the description for the 1,732 tiny shatters your life has become after someone lobs a cannon into the Center that grounds you.

Many of the people who were generous enough and courageous enough to share of themselves in this book, their music, their creative work, were traumatized as children. The potential that was "forever" dwelt in that moment, hanging in the balance between delight and despair. Innocence lost in that moment; and the nubbin of courage emerged through the snow.

> I never betrayed why I was sensitive. I sure as hell wasn't going to expose myself to potential ridicule by telling them about how shattering my experiences as a child had been as a result of my ear and deafness.
>
> (Stanley, 2014, p. 114).

The Children of No Before. The Children building themselves a world from the shards of one they didn't know, didn't understand.

Could never know. Because their Brains were changed, and their world, Our world, was a very different place.

There is a common theme here, and it is that this time, it really is "all about you." I talk about what it is "for me." I include the confusion of not understanding how my few friends who do not have cognitive differences are so positively and comfortably sure that their brains function as undifferentiated "wholes."

This is how it looks to me. This is what I feel, especially when I am on the edge of a traumatic break. These are not what are happily called "psychotic breaks." A "psychotic break" is when someone loses touch with reality.

This is different. This is when my physical self is in one place, usually where there are crowds of people or the musical potential for triggers.

And I know I am here. Then, something gets triggered; *something* takes me to some place I've been before. It happens so fast, and so infrequently, that I can't feel the process. One minute I'm doing one thing, and the next there's a movie in my head. Because the brain doesn't distinguish sensory inputs from memories and Flashbacks as different from the current sensory inputs, I am, in a strange world, in two places at once.

I don't have time to carefully consider my "options." I just "go." At some point, my Mind does kick in, usually terrified and screaming something about the Two Places At Once paradox.

Interestingly, it's my Mind that becomes terrified. My Body very calmly goes about doing its job. That means assessing the situation using *only* sensory input. I can observe the process but it is usually happening so fast that nothing reaches the slower Cerebrum.

This shouldn't be strange to people. This way of living is what has caused us to survive as a species, long before our big brains came into existence. It's how we escaped large predators lurking in the prehistoric trees. It's the aroma – or the smell – of fruit that told us if it was safe to eat. I am going to risk saying that individuals who stopped to "consider their options" are no longer with us because their contribution to the gene pool disappeared in the stomach of the tiger who measured distance with her eyes and body, not stopping to "consider possible best options."

On a day when I was especially emotionally frail, having had a panic attack several days before, a friend and I were talking about how the brain and body work together. She joyfully announced to me that I could "overcome the set of programs of my body." Why would I want to do that?

People work for years to automate their playing. A popular understanding is that it takes 10,000 repetitions to achieve mastery. With this kind of capability, why would I want to destroy the programming to get somewhere... Where? Somewhere Where? This Body keeps me alive, keeps me safe, keeps me whole. Why On Anybody's Green Earth would I want to ruin that?

Given that the Body is its own special kind of Mind, let's look at what is often perceived as the real jewel buried here: the cognitive Mind. It's the "big human brain," which I think we may all be able to agree, does what is popularly called "thinking." A more accurate way to put it is, The

Mind makes up stuff. The Body doesn't make up stuff. It reads data directly in from its environment.

I use my Body and lower Brain a lot, but I keep my cognitive Mind in the corner in shut-up-ation, especially when I am processing things, Events. These are more about my physical responses than they are about how my Mind has storied the Event. And here is the critical focus: the Mind *creates* Story. The Event simply is what it is. Then, once the initial, physical responses are processed, the Emotions first becoming Feelings and from there, Stories. These Stories are what become "truth" for many. And, because they have elaborated "on the fly," changing the data in the process, they can't go back and reexamine.

My friend, without realizing it, was absolutely precise in indirectly describing what the research has detected: Emotions begin in the Body; after fight-or-flight processing is complete, the sensations make their way up through cognitive pathways. At some point, they become Feelings. And here, the busy little Mind, housed firmly and unrelentingly in the Cerebrum, begins to "make Story."

Making Story is a process. It is not pulling an absolute truth from "somewhere," although as songwriters we often do that with songs. We believe Songs are Alive, that they have their own volition. Songs tell their own stories.

Minds are not like Songs. Minds are nosy, yappy little things that always gotta be causing trouble. Or, at least, that how my Mind is.

If it seems unusual, somewhat uncommon that I configure my brain parts this way, remember that "who I am," "how I am," is all I have ever known. There is no comparison between, "Well, this is how I do things now," and, "This is how I used to do it *before*." I am a Child of No Before. For Me, and many of my friends, We don't have what people like to call *prior* experiences. Essentially, everything is Now.

What's even more interesting is that one Cognitive Behavioral Therapeutic (CBT) approach is to focus on the Now. We are *always* focused on the Now. It's rudely called hypervigilance. Hypervigilance, the real skill, is what you develop when your life depends on monitoring the situation around you. Always.

My Story

Making my way through because I didn't realize there were any other alternatives. When I was eight my grandfather left us quietly one night.

He was my one real connection to the world. I went berserk. To hear people tell it, as I have no memory of this Event at all. My mother couldn't be bothered with a child experiencing the most important loss of her young life. The most intense emotional hurt. She had me sedated for the three days until after my grandfather was buried.

Reconfiguring

I wondered before writing this about the Elton John song, "The One," where he sings about how when you meet the person who is meant for you, all the pieces just fall into place. And all I could think of was, What the hell happened to all the other pieces? Seriously: New stuff arrives; what happens to the old stuff? This is a really good question... old stuff isn't a problem. It's the "new stuff" arriving in the middle of the not-yet-gone old stuff.

And this is potentially a problem. I think. Really. I do think it's a problem because then you have layers of pieces and some (shhh, maybe even many), of them have unfinished business.

A friend asked if I "remembered" anything from the Event at 18 months. I said, Not really. What I really meant was *not cognitively*, meaning I couldn't tell an authentic word-story. I make the distinction because My Body certainly could, and it could tell stories. In those stories I fell from road bridges where the roadway itself had disappeared and I was clinging to beams, crawling slowly across, usually nearly naked even in the cold. Sometimes I would fall. Sometimes I would wake screaming.

The nightmares became less frequent with time, reappearing infrequently now. But the fear of heights lasted well into adulthood, exhibiting itself as inability to cross bridges if I were walking, paralytic fear of looking down from high places. Just a whole bunch of inconvenient stuff that made outings sometimes treacherous.

It lasted until a trip to Bandelier National Forest, where I faced a choice at the ceremonial cave 200 feet up. My friend was going up. I was dithering. This pathway was tiny steps carved in rock, very old wooden ladders, in short, lots of places to lose one's footing.

I dithered. I reasoned. It was a choice between the fear and what might be a chance in a lifetime experience.

This is reconfiguring, for me: I want something bad enough to put myself out to get it. I wanted somehow to look out from that cave and experience the vista. But to get there, I had to stifle a long-standing fear and make it up that rickety, scary, ascent.

I did it.

In this fashion, every day is composed of new little journeys that make up the big Journey. Those are the words that tell you what I see: little globes of tiny journeys all bonded together in a stream, like in the picture below.

Exit, Stage Left: How extreme …

… do you need to be?

The concept of days filled with tiny globes of happenings, like completely enclosed worlds, clear, colored, transparent but contained, keeps morning from blending with – or contaminating – lunch, afternoon, dinner, depending on the intensity of the flow.

As you experience these events with Us, the highs the lows, the start-overs… and the amazing, magnificent search-and-destroy missions where We figure out how to turn a response We don't want into something We do: me and Aly dealing with loud sounds. On September 20th, 2023, Aly and I were chatting about our reactions to sound.

As I was saying: as you experience these generously shared lived experiences, you will be tempted to let your brain disbelieve, to say to you: This is too horrible, too outside anything we understand. It can't be true!

Trust me: It's true. Both what you might label, might *want* to label, "the good and the bad." For Us, it's just another walk in the park.

But given that people, human people, not "participants," not even patients, are locked in situations where the few existing escape options seem insurmountable. What do they do?

An acquaintance tells the horrifying story of killing the man who was trying to rape her. When she was 13. The overwhelming sense of the Event itself startles the Body to tears, to a profound sense of wonder about how You live through something like that. It's better that I cry than that I think about it. It's better to let my Body feel the empathetic pain than that I decide how I might feel about it; that I stop My Mind from making Story.

In a lot of ways, it's hard to share what We have seen, what We have done, what others have done that We were a part of in some way, because We re-experience the Events, the Emotions, the Feelings, often what We saw, heard, felt physically. And this hurts. The Memories hurt. The wishing things had somehow been different hurts. The things, the people, the opportunities We have lost or ruined before We developed the ability to save ourselves from even greater disaster, these also hurt.

Someone I was once close to, a brilliant but tragic human being, killed a dealer in a drug deal gone bad. The scene is a darkened room, moonlight streaming in, where she sat, waiting, gun in her hands. Childhood trauma had led her here. She was always living on the edge, challenging danger. Anything to stop the incredible disappointment, the rage she felt toward her father, the resentment she felt at her family's circumstances because of her father's ways. Afterwards, or maybe it was simply a continuation of what had begun early in her life, her adult life was a series of shattered relationships, the last of which ended in her own murder.

I wonder how many traumatic Events occur when individuals are in situations they suddenly can't get out of. What did these two people have to do? To save their lives, they shattered the workings of Body, Brain, and Mind.

What do we do when we can't get out? I tried to kill myself a couple of times. When that didn't work effectively, I was forced to begin to learn, to understand, to have a conversation with the various "parts" that were participating in the responses to the shock, the fear. I am very clear in describing the responses as *the* responses, not *My* responses, because clearly the resulting emotions and behaviors were not what I would have chosen.

Many of Us were caught in those "in between a rock and a rock" places. Where you listen and you say, Oh fuck that sucks. Because it does; it really does. You see it, they see it: you both know it really sucks.

So sometimes, you take measures to "get out" that seem "extreme" from other points of view. But think more deeply about what "getting out" might mean. Did you imagine escaping from jail, escaping from a madhouse, escaping from a rapist? Show hands: How many knew it was more often escaping from your own mind? Thought so.

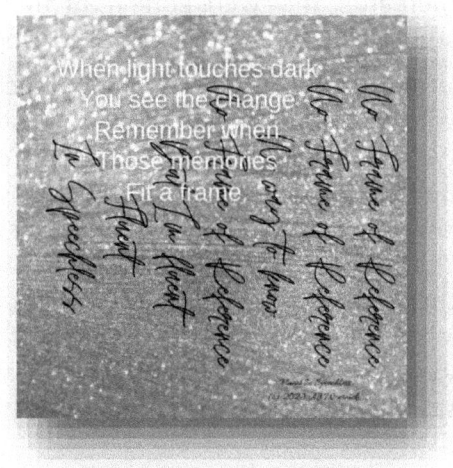

What's "Out?" Where's "Out?"

There's something very important here about having a place to go back to and I can't quite pinpoint what it is. But the line keeps playing "*About having a place to go back to; About having a place to go back to.*"

I don't understand because I don't have a place to go back to. I don't have a place, I don't have a time when I was "me" before I became Me. But I remember the music. When many people remember the happy – or not – events: gatherings, parties, trips, I remember the songs. My dad played harp, a small harmonica that he always had in his pocket. My dad didn't have a genre; he had songs that he liked. *Cherry Pink and Apple Blossom White* was probably his favorite.

Other people, famous musicians, have turned to music to explore, to struggle with, and to cry out the tears, and pain, and the rejection, the denial. The rejection, the denial, are real. It lurks like a special kind of hatred, socially sanctioned.

One day, I read what I think is the most emotionally gripping story in this book, of the little girl sliding down the slate roof on her face. The two people, both of whom I had known for 22 years, shrugged, had no comments. Unpleasantly stunned, I thought, Who are these people? Who am I hanging out with? Are they just the husks of souls? Shortly thereafter, they were gone from my life, banished for their inexplicable, stunning, actual unwillingness to recognize the humanity in others.

And so the voices with more reach, more volume – sometimes any volume at all – are important in Our struggle to be known as the people We are. Yep, bad things happened. Yep, some of Us will never recover. But then, some of Us will. My job is simply to love Us enough, long enough, that We begin to love Ourselves. My job is not to love the "haves," the "entitleds," the "unbrokens" as much as They think I owe them, as much as They think They should have first pick at the table. My job is to love Us, the often broken, often lost, often scared, to share My view of how it looks from the inside, so there is Validation, the kind that says, "I see me in that story. If those people can grow after all that, I can too."

Views From A Larger World

I came to write this section, multiple times, because understanding this emotionally, as part of what I and my friends do, would reduce me to tears, quite literally, and I would be unable to go on. I would think of what We actually struggle with: the anxiety, the fear, the disorientation, so many things.

And when I learned more about what famous musicians coped with, I was again overwhelmed with sadness. This continued for weeks: Opening; crying; closing.

One night in a bar in the town that changed its name for the money, my dear and becoming dearer friend Jamie, who wrote the amazing *Va-Va-Voom* was talking about the struggle, not his but about how he saw it. Something bothered me about the story. There wasn't anything particularly odd about the story. I had heard it dozens of times from different people. But mostly what it was, was that it didn't match how I saw it, on multiple levels.

He was telling me the story of one of our friends, and it was all about the "bad stuff," the challenges. I knew this person as a brilliant musician, someone so incredibly skilled that it's difficult to describe, difficult to reference. He plays the most wonderful, non-repetitive solos that take you on a beautiful journey through his musical dreams. I wondered. I still wonder, How do people not see this?

And then I knew: People are blinded by the stories that paint Us as "helpless victims." They see the terrible things that happened and are grateful it didn't happen to them. The introduction to an interview with Lady Gaga promises to shed light on the "paradox." That perceived paradox was the storied conflict between her success and the strong belief that people with PTSD are unable to do impressive and successful things (Wisdom Living 101, 2023).

And then I saw it: My sadness, my unwillingness to approach this chapter was occurring because I had read myself into the very trap I am so soundly against: Do Not paint Us as "helpless victims." And I realized, That's it! Yeah, the bad stuff happened. But look at what they did!

Highly successful actress Andie McDowell said, "I'm still working on my anxiety. It's hard to get rid of so much PTSD. It's in your bones and it's in your nervous system for sure."

Then she pauses. "But I look at the bright side: I can use it, I can tap into that." (Mechling, 2021)

She acknowledged that, yes, there were some problems, but that she had restructured them into skills. This is classic posttraumatic growth: you take the ways your Mind – it's always the pesky mind – is working, and figure out how it can be a useful tool. How can you use it instead of being beset by it?

The Music Born of Trauma

Musicians have always led the stories of what's what. And they have often told their stories in song.

The legendary Marvin Gaye's most famous song, *How Sweet It Is to Be Loved by You*, was released in November of 1964. It had been written by the very famous Motown writing team, Holland-Dozier-Holland. They wrote numerous sings for Motown artists including *Heat Wave*, recorded by Martha and the Vandellas in 1963, and then covered by Linda Ronstadt in 1975. *Run, Run, Run* was released in 1964 on The Supremes album, *Where Did Our Love Go*.

How Sweet It Is to Be Loved by You was inspired by Jackie Gleason's famous saying, How sweet it is. The Jackie Gleason Show first aired in 1949, when television was still black and white and depended on antennas. It was a time when Black music was poised to cross over into the White, teen-aged market. In the early days of modern music, it was very much a black and white thing. Labels targeted specific markets and those markets were seen and treated as isolated. It was in this world that Marvin Gaye celebrated his first number one hit, *I Heard It Through the*

Grapevine, in 1968. Overall, he had three #1 hits, released 54 albums, and 83 singles.

Marvin had serious problems with his parents starting when he was little. This is something so many of Us are familiar with. He said, "living with Father was like living with a king, an all-cruel, changeable, cruel and all-powerful king". (Eames, 2022) And then his dad killed him. On April 1st, 1984. With a .38 revolver. He was sentenced to six years, suspended, and five years' probation. Marvin would have been 45 the next day.

When I found out Marvin had been shot by his father, I immediately flashed to sound, image, vision, response: That could have been Me. Then a pause, and "Oh wait...".

Who Are We? The A Side

My conversation with Jamie provoked a whole new choo-choo of thought in my head: what is it that we expect from our parents when we are young children? Clearly, some of Us, a percentage can't even be suggested, have written Our parents off early on. How did We make those decisions? What kinds of conversations helped Us clarify Our thoughts? I know mine. Essentially simple: a string of broken promises. Others include never being good enough, never seeing the flash of approving, joyous smiles. The smiles that say, Do it some more, ok?

We all do various things in response. I did a version of cutting off my nose to stop the hurt. Others have developed interesting forms of isolation and estrangement. But really, I don't know.

There does seem to be some research on how children react to early caregiver behaviors, but none that expect children to develop adverse cognitive reactions to their caregivers. In other words, to make the difference as clear as possible, the research looks at how children behave after having experienced particular behaviors. I am asking, Do children have a set of standards, of expectations "built in" like in mitochondrial DNA? The mitochondrial DNA is how baby songbirds all know the specific song for their kind.

So do we, as children? A priori? (That means before the fact, like, before the craziness starts.) Somehow, my Mind believed that I was entitled to kept promises. Was I socialized to believe that? Did I feel it? I feel the disappointment, that's a Feeling, identifiable by its label.

But my decision was cognitive. I thought about it; I discussed it with both grandparents. But did I hear relatives gossiping at the kitchen table when they came to visit their parents: Such a beautiful child [hushed tones] too bad her dad couldn't make it? He should, you know *whisper, whisper.*

It's kind of a good story, that. Plausible, even but it's not the truth. The truth is that every time I heard my dad was coming, I was so happy. My spirits lifted, you might say. And then there was the anticipation: what time would he be there? What would we do?

Usually, this chattiness persisted up until the promised arrival time, when there was a canceling phone call, or he simply didn't show with apologies later. And each time, the letdown hurt. And It hurt more over time because I began to anticipate it. And finally, I reached my limit. No more: I stopped caring whether he came or not. Just like that. I made the decision and it was easy.

For Me it was easy because I had a Mind and I had a grandpa. We talked about so many things: the war; the politics; his adventures in the underground in the Ukraine and Poland, and in countries named flavor of the day as the battle lines raged. Other children were not so lucky. Other children had no one to help them make sense of the insanity. Later, My grandpa died so I had to move home to the raging battle lines there. To Hell. To Damnation. To No Way Out. So I know what it's like. Do I know what to do with the anger? No. The disappointment? No. The just plain sorrow? Maybe write a Blues song called Just Plain Sorrow. D sharp minor Blues with a half step rise as a surprise.

Of course, I was also a very shell-shocked child, peering out at the world with wary eyes, staying out of the way, invisible as much as possible. Hoping never to have to talk to anyone, never to have to participate in those well-meaning(?) soul-grinding conversations that began, "So, has your dad been down to see you?" I didn't know the word fuck then. I also didn't know how badly I needed it.

Even now, if I wonder how I was with people later on, I flash back to being small, in a dress that doesn't seem mine, someone is approaching, arms held out. I scream. I'm down. The obvious choice, of course, is to just not wonder about questions like that. But of course, every once in a while My yappy, pesky Mind sneaks out of its corner and turns on its own AI.

Who Are We? The B Side

So far, what I've shared probably seems pretty awful. But I am a songwriter: I paint my songs with words, choosing the rhythms, the meanings, the harmonics to make a "sound" that some people can hear and put music to. When that happens, it's a joyous thing.

I have a friend, and seeing him perform in Europe reminds Me that unlike ordinary people We don't "become whole different people." We appear and behave differently because that's the world We are in, body, mind and soul. We are nothing if not consistent. And this is who We are, at that moment, in that time. Places are different. Sounds are different. Possibilities and opportunities are different, depending.

So some contexts are full of Triggers for one or more of Us. Others are not. Where We go depends on who and what We want to play.

Some of Us play various things, sometimes whole collections of musical instruments, sometimes people's heads. I have a close friend. We do this together. We can't be all that terrible because no one has taken that much deserved retribution on Us. But, yeah, We have developed very keen, intuitive skills that give Us acute insight into others, especially ordinary people. Musicians will frequently see it coming, see Us do it. Anticipate and return volley. Some will not, but a lot will. Ordinary people, on the other hand, will take everything at face value and miss the multilevel subjokes. Subjokes are created by connected references, for example, whistling *Windy* by The Association when someone says, Gee it's really blowing out there today.

So, level 1 is the first statement. Level 2 is the whistling; three is the name of the band. And four is the name of the song. This is a simple example of the kinds of connections we make easily because of two things, really. One is the way Our minds are now structured. They have changed, but we don't really know how.

And the second is that what We do know, and know really well, is how to use those changes for all kinds of things, mostly to have fun, I would hypothesize. Based on my not very broad but distinctly detailed personal experience. The other night, at the bar In the town that changed Its name for a million bucks, I was gifted with the words for what I knew, understood: The PTSD, it never goes away, really. But We have a lot of fun with it, some of Us. I have synaesthesia; some of my friends do also. I am also sound-dependent where most people are sight-dependent. I struggle to remember faces; it's called prosopagnosia. Face blindness for

Us humans. I recognize people by their voices; at the same time, I sense how they are. I can do a lot the same thing by looking at people's bodies. The term body language doesn't tell you about all the sublime details that go into making these exquisite determinations. It's a unique kind of authenticity.

So to summarize, We are generally highly skilled in some ways that to Us are just what We do, but don't seem that way to others. Many of us are gifted to the extreme. Many of Us have little patience with the boringness that permeates other people's lives. But then, We have wonderful obsessions that I might suggest others might find equally boring. I, for example, have been known to work on one song for six or seven hours.

What "They" Say

Returning to the original question: How do We develop "expectations," those expectations that will eventually dictate how We handle the Trauma assailing Us? Outside, in the academic community, there is a significant amount of research on a different perspective of what young children expect from their parents and how they develop these expectations. Different types of investigations in Developmental Psychology have looked at how children form expectations of their parents and family dynamics. But these are after the fact. After all the parental/care giver behaviors, good and bad, have been done, how do the children behave? Does anyone ask if they are traumatized?

Popular research studies have "examined" how different ways of Our being treated by Our parents show up in Our behavior later. Parental behavior is supposed to have shaped Our "expectations." (Toof, et al., 2020) ChatGPT reported research consensus that "Parental warmth, affection, and consistent responsiveness have been associated with positive child outcomes and the development of secure attachment, while inconsistent or harsh parenting can lead to insecure attachment and negative expectations of parental support." (Retrieved 11/26/2023). But We are simply the objects if the research. Sadly. Once again. Silenced by bias.

4: Posttraumatic Growth

The small child slid down the slate of the Victorian roof on her face, tearing skin, slicing into flesh. Then, a muffled thump as her tiny 18-month-old body landed headfirst on the concrete below. The neighbor lady downstairs saw a doll fly past and rushed out the door to get it, to return it to the angel upstairs. But. Not a doll: Instead, the tiny, golden-haired Angel lay unmoving in a widening pool of blood.

Tossed unceremoniously through that high casement window by her mother.

And so it begins...

Where do you go from here? What starts the journey? I recall desperation, loneliness, not understanding. I recall searching inside myself for a way to stop hurting. I was four. And a half. In this moment, the parents who lived on the other side of town and rarely came to visit became "non-essential" to my life as I simply. Stopped. Caring. I was four. And a half. I had already lived a lifetime and it wasn't over.

These chapters share the sounds, words and feelings of the musicians who have created them. They are all my friends. They all volunteered into the creation of this book. They have all coped with loss, and struggle in some way. Sometimes, as musicians, We write not so much for ourselves as for others, for others to know, to feel, to see new vistas – or old ones in different ways.

In Chapter 5 we talk about the many uses of Edges, the many ways it can be defined, and importantly, why Edges tell the careful observer when We have maxed out Our comfort level. Edges are songs; they have messages that are meant to be understood.

As people we are never more vulnerable than when we are crafting the Music of Love. But the Music gives us a whole different language AND ways to say intimate things that we wouldn't be able to say face-to-face. Many of Us are introverted and introspective. The introspection gives Us up-close and personal experiences with Our Emotions and Feelings. Introversion makes it less likely that We will share the beautiful understandings We have crafted in Our conversations with Our own

Minds. But Music lets us put all if these together in ways that We can share.

And I know I often wonder, What is it like for others? What do you feel when you anticipate seeing me? Holding me? Taking me to your secret place, to your heart?

Brother from Another Mother

Paul Stanley – The Starchild of KISS – has to be the poster boy for personal growth after grinding social and emotional trauma. Born deaf in his right ear, and also missing the external cartilage, he was tormented by schoolmates. He received no support at home, a place where he also hated to go, and where he was constantly scrutinized and criticized. He writes in his book, Face the Music: A Life Exposed, that it was his "sense of self-preservation and an urge to improve [him]self always overrode any other impulses" that enabled him to become the success that he has. He also writes about how he realized that being famous, being rich, didn't fill the hole inside him. That required a different kind of work.

I see myself in his story, growing up isolated but for different reasons. But particularly, because, like me, he has lived with his trauma all his life. That means that like me, he has no memory of a life before the trauma. I wonder what brains do when in social situations, for example, it reaches for the experiential memory that never surfaces.

And now you're workin' your way out of a bad place.

Creativity and The Great Escape

When I am stuck in a place, it doesn't matter what kind, I use what I'll call cognitive resources to figure out a solution that gets me past the stuck point. I am using the term cognitive resources where you would maybe think that I would say "brain" or maybe "mind" because pretty soon, I am going to take you on a tour of my head, of how I think.

When I was a child, many times the situations were, to me, unbearable. No amount of mentally searching for escape options of the more practical kind presented themselves as plans that might actually work. I devised plans for hiding in plain – and sometimes not so plain – sight. I was aiming for a kind of transparency that I never quite achieved.

At the same time that I was trying to develop my teleportation skills, I began writing stories and learning songs. I didn't think about them. These were just things I did; they were who I was.

But who I was, on the outside a tiny, blonde, seven-year-old girl, on the inside was now independent of the social context around her. When at home, she lived totally in a world of her own making. A situation that brings its feelings with it as I write about myself in third person. As I feel the space, the distance, the silence.

Over time, things got worse, the war zone more dangerous and the simple process of absenting myself with alcohol became an option. It wasn't a workable one. But before the alcohol, before the drugs, there was the music that I so desperately hoped would be an SOS, a desperate call for help; the endless pleas in the way I played Beethoven, especially Beethoven. Chopin. Rachmaninoff. Pieces that, under my fingers, would scream how I felt; would send the feelings of helplessness, of the loss of hope, into the Universe.

But as creative as I was in my musical expression, no one came. The music pleaded, begged. Wanted. Just a little hope. None came.

I asked my uncle about it one day. After the blood had been cleared; the house abandoned. He said, quite smugly, actually: I don't interfere in another man's household. I lost every positive emotion I had for him that day. To think that his belief system, his male pride, was more important than the well-being of three defenseless children. So people will want to say: Oh, but that's how things were back then. Don't go there.

Tears in Heaven

Everyone is familiar with Eric Clapton's heart-rending Tears in Heaven, his ethereal expression of his loss of his son. The song is not "about" his loss; the song *is* his loss; it *is* his pain. It is his only recourse to connect with the world, with life, after unbelievable tragedy, tragedy the DSM-III liked to say was "generally outside the range of usual human experience."

Yes, when your four-year-old son falls 53 stories to his death, that is probably "outside the range of usual human experience." But, he did the only thing a musician can do in that situation: he wrote a song to carry his feelings. In 1993, *Tears in Heaven* won Grammy Awards for both song and record of the year.

What is "Creativity?"

Creativity is what people call it when other people are able to make something no one has ever seen before. KISS is certainly emblematic of that idea. The works of the great composers and geniuses like Lou Reed,

David Gilmour, David Bowie. The technology that supports us is also massively creative, from the microphones to tablet-based sound boards, to the digital audio workstation software that makes astounding recordings possible, ours is a world drenched, not in a static creativity but in a creative flow.

That's the "outside" view of creativity. The inside view is how We make Our way through each. And. Every. Day. Some days are good; We can glide through them like a hot knife through butter. Other days: Not so much.

Fortunately for Me, not only is my wide range of emotions known to my inner circle, but We all share the same issues. We don't like crowds because most of Us are also empathic. This means that We absorb the way others are feeling. Some people would say, "pick up on" but that is a cognitive result. It means that there was enough time for the Emotions to be processed through the Cerebrum and so become Feelings. That there was enough time for the sequence to be made into Story, to be translated into words others might grasp.

That's not the way it works in crowds. In crowds, We are monitoring. We are watching and evaluating everything for its safety level. When We are doing this, We are not able to screen what Our bodies are sensing. And then, eventually, We reach overload.

One of my very close friends will crash with a panic attack when this happens. An astounding performer, totally safe when she is on stage, is also totally vulnerable when she's not. We all understand this and We know to just hover while she makes her way back up. If she calls, We answer. If We don't hear from her, We text support. She is the most vulnerable among Us and We protect her. Because We can. But We work on a rule: Stay out of my face while I'm healing me. Especially don't touch me.

Courage, Bravery and Empowerment

Two researchers, Calhoun and Tedeschi (1999), have researched the phenomenon where people who have experienced significant traumas on a range from positive to negative, grow in ways that enrich them. They learned that feeling more powerful, more able to survive, was a common theme among those who had faced major challenges and survived. The people went on from their experience, not to say that their PTSD was cured, but that they survived and thrived. At the time there was no name for what was truly a phenomenon. Today it's called Posttraumatic Growth.

A recent book by Jim Rendon, entitled Upside: The New Science of Posttraumatic Growth, said the following when discussing a man named Mullins, who had been in a very debilitating car accident.

> Such a severe accident, the kind that leaves one with lifelong struggles, is not supposed to change a person in such a positive way. Drunk driving accidents should not transform a high school dropout and a block layer to a person who puts on suits and makes presentations. But that is Mullins's story.
>
> (p. 68)

Having survived a head-on collision with a cement sidewalk, I was really curious as to who might have unfeelingly condemned Us to lives with no hope of anywhere or anyhow else to be. Who would be so cruel?

Somehow a background story emerged that became popular and pervasive, it seems. It was that people who had undergone Events at the DSM level of being "Generally outside the range of usual human experience" were or should be *expected* to be miserable, crippled mentally, physically, and emotionally. (I guess). And while I find this "interesting" in a somewhat less flattering way, it is nonetheless a view that I see reflected in the majority of the published research on PTSD.

The work of Tedeschi and Calhoun introduced an aberration: people were not supposed to make their way out of darkness. When The Starchild sings about the many things he wants to do "in the darkness," it's supposed to be in a simple song about a rock star and someone he is spending time with. But I could never pass that line smoothly; there was always something deeper, poking, saying "there's more here." Stanley Bert Eisen, born without an external right ear and deaf because the ear canal was closed, through sheer determination, courage, believing in his and Gene's ability to do anything they set their minds to, became arguably the most recognizable front man in rock history for the most successful rock band in history. I think this is not supposed to happen. I think that's what people believe.

And so, when Tedeschi and Calhoun named this "impossible" phenomenon, named it *Posttraumatic Growth*, it sparked a frenzy in at least psychology and psychiatry because it challenged the prevailing attitude. The concept, and more importantly, the *direction*, the possibilities, and the hope was announced in the mid-nineties. It challenged the popular – and lucrative – focus on the *pathology* after trauma, that is, on what We call the symptoms.

Calhoun and Tedeschi (1999) proposed, based on substantial research, that trauma could be the change in thinking that could lead to the observed impressive personal growth. This is a little awkward. What it more likely should say is that Trauma may be the catalyst for changes in how the brain processes its inputs. This distinction is important especially in PTSD because in extreme cases where danger is present, my Body is in motion before my Mind has realized it will need to deliberate.

Research believes that it has captured the timing and sequences of brain reactions. There are two limitations. The first is that substantial numbers of the recent reports note that their participants were what are called convenience *samples*. These are groups of people who are easy to recruit; college sophomores in Psychology are a popular choice. Another important characteristic is that the people do not come from what's known as a "sensitive population." These require special procedures to ensure the people participating are not harmed or taken advantage of. And these cause extra work, so researchers will avoid them as much as possible.

Paradoxes, Losses, and Gains

Tedeschi, Calhoun, and Grolieu (2015) wrote that *"There appears to be a basic paradox that is apprehended by trauma survivors who report these aspects of posttraumatic growth, that their losses have produced gains."*

I don't know if paradoxes exist in Nature, but its appearance in this particular case pretty directly suggests that the concept of "loss" needs to be examined critically.

But curious, I said to ChatGPT: "*good morning. do actual paradoxes exist in nature?*"

> Today, 11:31 AM
>
> good morning. do actual paradoxes exist in nature?
>
> Good morning! Paradoxes are generally constructs of language or human thinking rather than physical phenomena. They typically arise when our understanding or representation of a situation involves contradictions or conflicts with intuition.

Essentially this is saying that paradoxes, which make us uncomfortable, make us feel like We should be doing something, are places where We need to look deeper, start to understand the texture and the terrain of the situation. Over time and many discussions, people were beginning to notice that PTSD was more complex than they had previously hoped.

But what I find odd here is that Tedeschi et. al find this concept troublesome. They needed to label the possibility of growth after trauma "a paradox:" generally two conflicting ideas or beliefs that are both held to be true simultaneously. Thus researchers have storied Us as *broken, useless,* and *incurable,* because it's simply not possible in the way society conceptualizes the world – Our "worldview," Our "weltanschauung," – for it to be possible that We will now experience anything other than pain and suffering. It's really all about how We are storied.

What is "Loss" in PTSD?

Since I and most of my friends don't have a "Before," that is, We have lived with the fallout of often multiple traumas since essentially birth, We don't have actual concepts of losses. The clinically reported losses seem to be more oriented towards traumatic events occurring sometime after people have begun their grown-up lives.

The Loss list of General Understanding is:
   1. Loss of a sense of safety and security

2. Loss of trust in others
3. Loss of a positive worldview
4. Loss of personal identity
5. Loss of relationships or social connections
6. Loss of control or agency
7. Loss of a sense of belonging
8. Loss of self-esteem or self-worth

From my perspective, it's difficult to lose something that you never had. It's true that We don't have these things identified as "losses:" We don't often have, for example, a sense of belonging because We don't know *how* to belong. We never learned; We never had the chance. I, personally, did eventually lose my trust in my father, lost my steadfast belief that he was my "whatever good dads are supposed to be."

In the long run, my very practical solution – to simply stop caring – was very destructive. Not caring was my go-to response for everything. It was fast, clean, easy. And lead to an inaccurate personal narrative. It was an unconscious combination of some of the nastiness spewed by my mother in particular, and the outsider views of both my coldness and erratic behavior. These were storied as "who I was" and the implication always was that I should be something different and it was my *fault* that I wasn't.

The Broad Scope of Gains from Losses

The fact that some of us have changed lives, better lives even, that result from some of the most horrific events known to humankind, is not a "paradox." It is simply a stupid idea held by a research community that tends to specialize in the production of papers that fatten the résumés that lead to tenure, grant money, and often, consultancies. If the research focused more on facing the issues rather than filling their coffers, the world might be a better place entirely.

Gains and Losses

The concept of gains resulting from losses is not new and is broad in scope. Financial losses can spur people to learn more about financial management, which can lead to better decisions and hence more wealth. In a concept called "Investment Rebalance," investors buy "losing" assets at a lower price and then see gains when those assets "recover," that is, return to their more consistent performance. Other examples are tax write-offs, dramatic changes in business strategy, often with dramatic innovation. Netflix is a great example of this: It moved away from DVD rentals that had to be received and returned by mail to their current streaming service.

Personal Development

Personal gains tend to be less physical and more about personal growth in some way. When people are faced with losses, this can deepen their emotional resilience, and because they have to strategize their way out, or through, they emerge with a better understanding of themselves, of who they are.

There is also a viewpoint that says that every loss, every failure, every setback is a new chance. They're chances to plan a different pathway, learning from the weaknesses of the previous attempts. They're chances to do a complete about-face and learn something new, something exciting, challenging.

Or, as in the collection process in electronic games, they're chances to develop skills, and acquire tools and resources that will help in the future.

And in these times, there's that old bugaboo, job loss. This is an opportunity to consider doing something you really want to do, something you're passionate about.

Physical Losses

Finally, there is the reality that physical losses, like amputations, or the loss of hearing or sight, can be devastating, but can lead to amazing breakthroughs.

There is psychological resilience, where incredible mental strength is needed to sustain the hard work necessary to readjust, to develop new ways of being, of moving, of trusting one's body. The person who went into this is different than the one who came out the other side.

Some physical losses can lead to improved physical and mental health. Diabetics, for example, often have to have portions of their feet removed to prevent infection and gangrene. An indirect result of such bodily losses is the vast increase in prosthetics technology. These advances continue marching forward long after the initial trigger is forgotten.

The Rewards of "I did this"

There are gains in one's outlook on life, and these can result from that incredible feeling of making it through. One day, you are sitting there, and you look around, and it hits you: I did this!

And whatever this is, realizing that You Did It *rocks your day*. Along the way, you may have gained some new friends, developed a more benevolent attitude, or even become more sensitive to others' feelings.

So with all this common knowledge about how gains frequently and reliably result from hundreds of different kinds of losses, gains of all kinds also, why is it that only We have been consigned to the "no possible hope" bin; to triage code red. Who could be that cruel?

A Loss by Any Other Name

Losses: some major chunk of Us can't identify with this. Personally, I feel a distance from a sense, a feeling, or any idea of loss. Because I never had it to consciously "lose."

I think to lose something, you have to have a sense of what that *something* is to begin with.

Of the eight types of losses listed previously, only two apply to me. From the initial trauma, I lost the social connection to my mom and dad on a daily basis. I obviously still trusted my dad when I ran across that gurney and leaped into the air toward him, trusting him to catch me. Which he did. How he did must have been fueled by sheer terror because he covered a lot of ground to catch me. Before I fell. Out of the air. Again.

I lost my trust in him, the second of the two applicable losses, two and a half years later, after what seemed like his 57th visit cancelation. That's 15 cancelations a year. One every month and an extra one buried somewhere in each of three quarters. Fifteen times a year, reliably, you told your kid you were coming. Reliably, she waited, hoping this time would be different, that you would come. And reliably, the sometimes one and only scheduled visit for the month would evaporate into the dreams and wishes of a perpetually lonely child.

The remaining losses are ones that require a sense of orientation in the world. At 18 months, I didn't have a good grasp on this. At four and a half, I had no control, no agency. If I had had, I would have seen my dad more often.

I don't know if I ever had a sense of safety and security. I don't know what was happening with my parents before then. But clearly it was not good, and equally clearly, some things happened that could not be described as even remotely safe.

At four and a half, I did lose my sense of belonging, of belonging to what I thought of as "my family." I knew my grandparents were "family" but not quite the same way. And they felt distant from the little nucleus I was supposed to be in and be comfortable in. Yes, I thought all this then, once I stopped crying from the pain in my body, that incredible sense of a loss so enormous it doesn't fit into a category.

It was the first day my world tipped over on its axis. The day when north became south. It was the day I crafted a new personal identity, fired on the foundation that if I didn't care, it wouldn't hurt.

I hadn't much thought about how I viewed the world. From the stories my grandpa told, there was "good" and "bad" in the world and these had ranges and extremes. So I didn't have a worldview, really. Nothing to gain, nothing to lose. So in short, I was shattered. My world as I saw it had either never existed or had been destroyed. I didn't think of it as a "world" then. I was just *being* somewhere.

And this was the day that a belief that I was better than them began to emerge: I had thought I was a good child, an adorable child. Everyone said so. But that couldn't possibly be true: a paradox. Two opposite things held simultaneously to be true.

But I didn't automatically assume that I wasn't good, that I wasn't adorable. I knew I was. And I was born. And not under a bad sign.

When a child is unhappy, crying, you distract them with something. There was a river across the street, a river full of boulders and fish. I learned to try to catch a fish with an appropriately looped and twisted stem of grass as I learned world history. My grandpa had been a guide in the "underground railway" in Eastern Europe. It was scary and people died sometimes. But I loved those very stories that horrified my grandmother.

Views From the Outside

It's a struggle to survive in an environment, perhaps of Our own making, where We are comfortable being. And frequently, the stories that are written about Us present Us as victims. But since We are victims who can't be helped, We see shades of Tuskegee: "let's see what happens if..."

One paper advocated for "the emerging therapeutic application of ketamine" (Krystal, et al., 2017). Scary thought that. The authors open their discussion by saying that "PTSD might be a 'synaptic disconnection syndrome'." However, a review of the literature in Google Scholar did not produce any papers that used the term. While there are different types of synaptic disorders, there are apparently no other published academic papers that use the specific term "synaptic disconnection syndrome."

However, the authors note the "importance of this perspective for the emerging therapeutic application of ketamine as a potential rapid-acting treatment for this disorder that may work, in part, by restoring synaptic connectivity."

In other words, the authors need to create a verbal, hypothetical context to justify their suggestion that ketamine might be a good "novel therapeutic." Their article was a review of existing animal studies. The authors didn't actually *talk* to any people who had PTSD.

And the synaptic disorders they are referring to are often called synaptopathies. This word is derived from two Greek words: *synapto* and *pathies*. *Synapto* comes from the *synapsis*, which actually refers to the joining of specific types of cells, homologous cells, at the beginning of cell division. It has been generalized as "a joining together." *Pathies* comes from *pathos*, and follows along with the popular research habit of identifying the details of the storied "inescapable brokenness, of suffering, of disease." Simply, it means "some brain synapses are behaving badly," essentially what happens when the brain's communication channels are clogged or missing.

Here are some neurological synaptopathies:
1. Autism Spectrum Disorders, ASDs, which show up as social interaction difficulties and repetitive behaviors.
2. Schizophrenia: This generally occurs during adolescence, and is believed to occur because some "overactive pruning" of synapses gets out of hand and takes away too many synapses, so the brain has less than the number it needs.
3. Alzheimer's Disease is where the quality of synaptic connections degrades because beta-amyloid plaques, that is, stuff in the

synapse path, disrupts the normal sending and understanding of sensory input.
4. Parkinson's Disease is when something called "dopaminergic synapses" produce tremors and bradykinesia (slowed movement).
5. Epilepsy, where the balance of the synapses that excite and those that inhibit is disrupted in some way. (ChatGPT, retrieved February 27, 2024).

And many of these synaptopathies have genetic links. (Simmons, et al., 2023).

While it is true that some behaviors associated with PTSD resemble some of the truly pathological afflictions, that doesn't really justify giving people ketamine to prove an hypothetical point.

Since the things I had heard about ketamine were essentially that it was an animal tranquilizer, I turned to ChatGPT for a quick overview. These are the "commonly known" side effects of ketamine:
1. Nausea or vomiting
2. Increase in heart rate and blood pressure
3. Disorientation or confusion
4. Dizziness
5. Flashbacks to past traumas
6. Hallucinations or other changes in sensory perception

More severe but rarer side effects can include:
1. Serious changes in mood and behavior
2. Severe anxiety or panic
3. Flashbacks to past traumas
4. Allergic reactions, which may be severe and include rash, hives, difficulty breathing, or swelling of the face, lips, tongue, or throat (ChatGPT, October 30, 2024)

Curiously, these are many of the same symptoms common to PTSD. Clearly these researchers had given little thought to the "broader view" of the potential application of ketamine, so long as they were able to test their hypothesis that ketamine would "[restore] synaptic connectivity." They point to "ketamine as a potential rapid-acting treatment for this disorder." (Krystal, et al., 2018).

Views of Hope

In contrast, the U.S. Veterans Administration has sponsored the development of a number of mobile apps aimed at helping veterans learn more about PTSD, and importantly, learn to manage their symptoms.

According to Weingardt & Greene (2015), these apps provide help and information in three different ways, and cover a wide range of needs. There are self-help; therapeutic help; and, record access. The self-help group is apps like PTSD Coach, Mindfulness Coach, and Parenting2Go.

The therapeutic help group consists of apps such as CBT-I Coach, PE Coach, and CPT Coach. They are designed to be used in conjunction with therapy. Neither of these two categories of mobile apps have any data sharing with the VA.

The record access group of apps allows veterans to download their medical records, order prescriptions, and make appointments. Because of their interactive nature, they share data with the VA and require the creation of valid accounts before access to the tools is granted.

These apps represent a move away from the obsession with pathologies, and most importantly, a move away from the destructive focus on Our brokenness and into the light of posttraumatic growth. Weingardt and Greene (2015) note: "This deliberate emphasis on skill development and planning, rather than healing and recovery, was designed to enhance the appeal of the course to the veteran and military audience." (p. 1)

A New View ... and Results

The new point of view facilitates the creation of new narratives, stories that people can tell of being more personally powerful, more able to manage their behavior through greater knowledge that leads to greater understanding. The new narratives talk of agency, the ability to have a firm and definite hand in recrafting a new life.

Historically, I knew I could be unpredictable, and that unpredictability seemed to stem from equally unpredictable events. I was impatient; often hated the world; and had absolutely no clue what was wrong with me. Finally, one day, a friend with a lot of experience with veterans said to me, You have PTSD. And like in the Elton John song, *The One*, the pieces all fell into place.

Knowing was the single greatest revelation of my entire challenged life. And I was happy to finally know that I wasn't who I was in my story. And now I knew that I could change My Story. I could find out who I was as a person when I was not saddled with unpredictable behaviors that seemed to have no rhyme or reason. An acquaintance echoed this sentiment. He said that knowing gives you the power to learn about what it is: out of the darkness and confusion and into the light.

5: The Maze of Edges

Edges are courage in the face of risk, in the face of adversity.

Edges are the stands We take on the paths to our personal authenticity. The Edges of the windows We open to greater views, greater worlds, greater being in the moment. Most of us walk on those Edges, Edges of the tension holding fear and wonder separated by the space between. Bobby was the pure essence of Edge. Endlessly charming, enormously kind, sometimes dramatically startling, he always had that Bobby Edge in the way he moved.

Edges are what keep Us from falling into darkness. Edges are what seem extreme to ordinary people because they are the last bastion of safety, the last chance to turn around. The last chance to think it over. Last chance to consider the power of love. They are the "last" at that moment in time. The last barrier before the cliff drop.

Edges are what keep Us from falling into darkness. Edges are what We do; they are how We think; frequently, they are how We feel, how We have storied Our Emotions. They are even Emotions We have and those that We have denied out of existence one way or another.

Edges are what keep Us from falling into darkness. They are the tools, tips, tricks, and sometimes simply interesting behaviors that give us time to process, prevent meltdowns, and escape when necessary.

Bobby's command of body language was brilliant and it showed not only in the way he moved but also in the way he understood people. And it showed in his playing.

Edges are sound. I can usually hear them coming down the road like Black Dogs. And like Black Dogs, you never know their emotional placement *at that moment*. Emotional placement is like Music: it changes colors, intensities, it rises, falls, turns back on itself. It swirls and flows. We are closely related to Music. Although, We really sometimes wonder, Do We have it? Or does it have Us?

You don't wanna tell
And it screams in your head
But you just got no one
　To tell
Anyway...so
It doesn't matter.
Who's gonna understand
　Those Feelings that you had.
Who's gonna care
　That you hurt

Aly and I have conversations about our Musics of Survival. It's where We go, what We do when "it gets bad." That's a euphemism for "Events that range from Overloaded to fully fledged Crash & Burn." While We all process this differently, what seems to be fairly consistent is that We all go to our hidey-holes. Places where We are free of noise, stress, most especially people, where We can heal. And there, We write, We compose, We dream.

This passage from a popular book just begins to tell what happens to people. It's really characteristic: you were in one world that you thought you knew and understood and then, you weren't. And you have to learn to cope with that. How you do that is your choice, because that world has taken up residence in your head, there's "no rhythm," there's "nothing predictable," there's "nothing you can count on at all."

"I've worked with a lot of people who have," she said. "And what they tell me is that when you've been in combat... what you've done, honestly, is left this world. You've left the world that you and I are in right now and walked into hell. ... It's chaos, and the chaos could start at any moment or end at any moment—there's no rhythm to it, nothing predictable, nothing you can count on at all."

(Kirkland, 2023, p. 86)

You don't need an actual war with guns and tanks, armies and navies, to be here: you simply need to be in the kind of impossible, unbelievable, inexplicable hell that others have an equally impossible, unbelievable, inexplicable way of turning your life into.

And yet, We make it through. That world never leaves, but it recedes, into the past, into memories less fresh, dulling more with time and the efforts We put in to manage, to cope. And for Us, coping often means Our music, Our songs, Our lyrics: the singularities and compositions that forge Our Stories.

Here is just a small sampling from Our musical hidey-holes, lyrics from songs written to help Us through Our nights, through wasted days, along vagaries of Our hopes and dreams, Our quest for Love, for understanding, and especially, Our struggle to avoid despair. We begin with Aly and her Journal.

Aly

When the pain in our Minds is so extreme, what do We do? We slash. We burn. Perhaps we throw children from windows. For Aly, this journal became a tunnel that later allowed her to see how far she had come. Written shortly before entering an inpatient program, she paints a vivid portrait of how We think, what We see, how We contextualize at critical junctures.

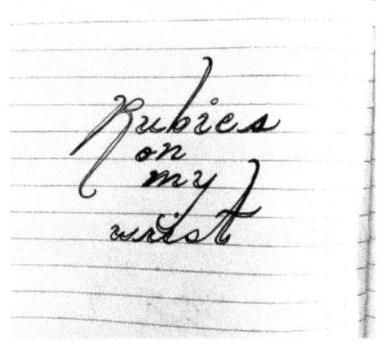

Rubies on My Wrist

I looked down

*I saw all of my
hopes and dreams lying
on the floor in a puddle
of blood.*

*My future was sprawled
out on the ceramic tile
swimming in a
pool that glowed ruby
red.
The white fluorescent
lights flashed glowing
brighter
The room was suddenly
20 degrees warmer*

I can't breathe

Then, What is the cost of isolation?

I saw that look

*I saw that look
In his eyes
The man I didn't know
The jacket I did*

*How far should I go in
Saying what I saw
From layers deep
Memories rise
Coalescing into vision*

*Blood river on the stark white floor
A single drop poised on the edge
Highlighting what was
Highlighting.
A single metonymy
Holding within its tiny self
Its speaking*

Its story

Eight-year history of a war zone
Each desperate cry and scream
Of love unfulfilled
Still here ricocheting around the walls
Rising to become the fog
That covers the ceiling in the second floor
A single drop poised. Above the river

Promising nothing.

The similarity in the critical imagery is startling. The first written by Aly, the second written by me. Written years apart, the dark blood stands in stark relief against white backgrounds. Both pieces start with an Event and in the streams of words swirl around the chaos. In *I Saw That Look*, images arise from history, a montage of perceptions, a tiny collection of Stories, maybe just one. Story.

Edges crystalize when Our fears, Our insecurities, Our hurts and Our drifting dreams are crystalized into courage by sheer force of Our tremendous wills, forces like what crystalized coal into diamonds. To understand the internal genesis of Edgy is to just begin to understand Our incredibly interesting relationship to Songs.

Sometimes, We write songs. We get an idea that inspires Us and We go. Other times, a lot actually, songs come to Us. All songwriters agree that this happens; others wonder what We are talking about, for the idea of a song "showing up" because it wants to be sung is completely unfathomable. The process is mysterious; I'm sure they think We are making it up. Not so, Grasshopper, not so.

Randy

Randy Lynch tells of the deep, dark depression that engulfed him during and after the break-up of his marriage. He went to work. That's it. No socializing, no outside activities, no connections to others. And then, literally out of the Brill Building in the Sky, where Lucy was the receptionist, song lyrics found homes with Randy. He had never written a lyric before. He had never had any plans to write lyrics, but, there they were.

At the time, Randy didn't play an instrument. Pressured by friends to share his lyrics, Randy bought a guitar, found a teacher, and today has released his first EP. Now he often says that Music saved his life.

He writes from the profound depth of the pain, his sense of loss, and a feeling of guilt that keeps him up at night. Dark thoughts and what-ifs; wishes and dreams that will never come true.

The chorus below, from *Too Long Sober*, is a lament that beautifully reflects his feelings. Using a drinking motif, he shares his happiness with his wife, when things were good, when they were together.

Too Long Sober

Back when
I'd get drunk
Kissing your lips
High as a kite
Just holding your hand
Loving you was a hell of a trip
And without you here
I'm so much colder
Now I drink till the night is over
Still I've been too long sober

Loving you was a hell of a trip

"Loving [her] was a hell of a trip," possibly the adventure of a lifetime.

In 10 lines, Randy has beautifully crafted the entire story of his relationship with his beautiful wife, whom he loved and lost and hopes to love again. These are the sounds of Edges, of that tension holding, in this case not the aforementioned fear and wonder, but instead happiness and pain, still separated by the space between that creates the bittersweet sensations that birth the song.

Haunted is the title track of Randy's new EP. Here he honors depths of pain of loss, of longing. He says, *And I take the pain... It's all I have left of her.*

Not wanting to give up the pain is a common though often unexpressed, unadmitted feeling. Whether the loved one has left turmoil and chaos, or died and We feel alone, We hold on to cherished memories. These memories don't fit into categories such as "good" or "bad." In our worlds, they qualify as intrinsic. They are essential to the completion of the Event. My dear friend Randy has made a world of his pain, his loss, and like the alchemists We are, he has transformed his understandings into beautiful Music that compels the listener – and the reader – to hear and understand.

Haunted

She haunts my days
And she keeps me up all night
She makes me pay
Though she's never in my sight

How can she be long gone
Left me all alone
But her memory   tortures me

She's in my mind
And I know I cannot run
She knows my crimes
I can't deny what I have done

And I take the pain
Don't want it to go away
It's all I have   left of her

She took my soul
And I'll never get it back
can't be whole
My world's burned away to black

My road to hell's been paved
I don't wanna be saved
I'm just content   to do my time

I'm haunted
I'm haunted
I'm haunted

Lost in the Rhyme

When every word I write is a song that reminds me of you

As Musicians, as Songwriters, We write because We must. We have no choice but to put what We feel, what We see, into word-sound-pictures that We can share with the world. We must, because We often find ourselves lost in the rhyme, lost in the stories, lost in the times.

Orrin

Orrin Wayland, O.B., has shared his song of not only lost love, but confusion around the relationship. *How could I have been so wrong*, he asks, in haunted words and gripping melodies.

Here is Orrin's story.

> "To me, music is not only sounds that can be put together to sound pleasing to the ear; music is an almost tangible manifestation of the emotions We feel deep down. Music is the sad feelings. It is the happy feelings. It is the melancholy feelings.
>
> "For my song, *Pictures*, when reading the words, or singing and playing it aloud, in my mind I can clearly see a dark Yellow. Sounds weird? Maybe. But that color, Yellow, means a lot to me. It is a feeling between sadness and joy. The space between what I Love and what I Hate. The gap that separates regret for the past and hope for the future. But each of those opposite feelings are all united under one commonality: the color Yellow."

Pictures

Saw some pictures that really bothered me
Don't know why they showed up on my feed
Don't really know what I should do
If I had a Time Machine I know I'd go back to you

Feel like I made the wrong choice once again cuz you were so much more than a friend
Was I in the wrong to let you go away
Guess we'll never know guess I'll never see the light of day

Are you happy happier now
Without me?
Sometimes I see your pictures you're always smiling
Why can't it be you and me?

Remember when you said that I was made for you?
Then I vanished into the wild blue
Let it go let it go that's what my friends say to me
But I just can't see

Are you happy happier now
Without me?
Sometimes I see your pictures you're always smiling
Why can't it be you and me?

I know I know maybe I was wrong
And I know I know you loved me all along
I know I know maybe I was wrong
And I know I know you loved me all along

Are you happy happier now
Without me?
Sometimes I see your pictures you're always smiling
Why can't it be you and me?

Often when We write, We see different things. We see how We Feel, what We Think. We learn how We were when We thought We were being something else. We see ourselves reflected in Our own minds as those reflections emerge through Our words.

Laura

Laura Bressan is a singer-songwriter living in Birmingham, UK. Originally from Italy, a small town in the Verona district, she has had the opportunity to work in multiple cultures in Western Europe and is fluent in Italian, French, Spanish and English.

She has a unique perspective here in that she views life through a very spiritual lens. She tells her story of perceiving that the world is much deeper than most suspect. She recognizes that her voice is a gift, her gift, and through exploration and appreciation, she has become a source of healing through sound. While she doesn't describe herself as a healer, it's well known that sound itself has healing properties. She tells her story herself in Chapter 8, The Sound Walk.

In *Changing Flavours*, she shares a coming-to-be Story. She shares her incremental movement toward trust, toward love, toward a precious kind of security.

In this and *Va-Va-Voom*, next, we begin to approach an understanding of what it feels like to come close to another person. These two songs are unique in their introspectiveness. They don't completely answer the questions, *What do you feel when you are about to hold me, to kiss me for the very first time?*

Frequently in songs we hear about longing or loss. It's not often that we hear about the shivers, the new perspectives, in some cases complete transformations. But here, we hear shivers from two different ways of experiencing the magnificence of Love.

Changing Flavours

Before the suspense of a stolen kiss
I found the comfort of your glance on me

And while I lingered on and on I finally opened back that door I kept closed for so long
My Life started
Changing Flavours
I slowly became aware of
How sweet kindness tastes
Of How a smile could change the sadness inside me

Slow and gentle you grew close to me
Wanting nothing but my company

And while I lingered on and on
I finally opened back that door
I kept closed for so long

My Life started Changing Flavours
I slowly became aware of
How sweet kindness tastes
Of How a smile could change the sadness inside me

My Life started Changing Flavours
The moment I saw you gazing At me, my Heartbeat Knew that we were meant to be
So I started to Believe My Life started Changing Flavours
The moment I saw you gazing At me, my Heartbeat showed me how this Life can be
So I started to Believe

BRIDGE
You must have felt just how I felt Acting like a mirror to my mind Your gaze took me far and far away
Endless choices and Futures
You showed me Who I can really Be!

CHORUS
My Life started Changing Flavours
The moment I saw you gazing At me, my Heartbeat Knew that we were meant to be
So I started to Believe
My Life started Changing Flavours
The moment I saw you gazing At me, my Heartbeat showed me how this Life can be
So I started to Believe

CODA/OUTRO
Believe (in me, in me)
Believe (in me, in me)
Believe (in me, in me)
So I started to Believe In Me

It's always so nice when a hope realizes itself. It's like they are little angels, little twinkling faeries, just waiting to become real. The next song by magician Jamie O'Hara exhibits just those characteristics of dreams that have come true, for this song was written after he and his beautiful wife had been married for some time.

Jamie

Jamie O'Hara is a magician, musician, songwriter, and wonderful entertainer and friend. He's shared this totally magical song, with an adorable twist – they said you drive a broom – embedded in what is otherwise a song of pure adoration.

Va-Va-Voom, performed by Jamie's band mate and long-time friend, Paul Walter Kimball, is a love song for Jamie's beautiful wife. Like all magical songs, it showed up and was finished in 15 minutes. This included the lyrics and the music.

This song also has what is probably my favorite line in all of Music: *An admission. Of submission.* Paul sings it as two lines, Jamie originally wrote it as one.

The line is contradictory of everything We have been told about ourselves, about who We are, and often about what We cannot do and be. We are not supposed to willingly, softly, gently submit to another person, even or maybe especially, in love. We are supposed to maintain our individual power; take stands; even battle for control, for decision making.

In the vision created in this song, we have options, we have choice. We can ignore the peer pressure from dead people that passes for "tradition" and we can instead connect with others. We can love safely, letting down our defenses and maybe most importantly, letting others love us in the most intimate ways: *An admission: Of submission.*

The words are little worlds unto themselves. The phrasing tells us that admitting to such a deep and vulnerable position is not a thing commonly done. Ditto for *submission*: a gentleness, a giving, a receiving softer, more private, more intimate. Different, and reserved for this one special person. We have a sense of "one special" for they often have a song that only we can hear. Uniquely, while We understand this so well among ourselves, the concept is totally inscrutable to ordinary people. While they hold firm on the concept of lots of fish in the sea, We know there is only one song.

Va-Va-Voom, or That's What I Say

Va-Va-Voom
Va-Va-Voom
It's what I say when you walk into the room
Va-Va-Voom
Va-Va-Voom
It's what I hear when you step into view
You got a walk that drives me wild
And a smile that makes me high
Oh gee can it be
Golly gee you got me.

Va-Va-Voom
Va-Va-Voom
You're the prettiest girl from here to the moon
Va-Va-Voom
Va-Va-Voom
Don't know why those other guys said that you drove a broom

You got curves that drive me crazy
And eyes that light the night
Oh gee can it be
Golly gee you got me
OMG and an acronym taking the Lord's name in vain
Can it be a question of authenticity
Golly gee an exclamation also taking the Lord's name in vain

*You got me
An admission
Of submission*

*Va-Va-Voom
Va-Va-Voom
You're like an oasis on a sandy dune
Va-Va-Voom
Va-Va-Voom
Like a cool rain on a hot afternoon
You got a laugh that makes me happy
And a twinkle in your eye
Oh gee can it be
Golly gee you got me
Va-Va-Voom
Va-Va-Voom
it's what I say when you walk into the room
Va-Va-Voom
Va-Va-Voom
it's what I hear when you step into view
 alright*

(Solo)

*Va-Va-Voom
Va-Va-Voom
That's what I say when you walk into the room*

*Va-Va-Voom
Va-Va-Voom
That's what I say when you walk into the room*

*Va-Va-Voom
Va-Va-Voom
That's what I say when you walk into the room*

*Va-Va-Voom
Va-Va-Voom
that's what I say when you step into view*

    Va-Va-Voom is a beautiful love song, a bit of a hard act to follow. In simply reading the words, we can feel the excitement of falling in love, see the light shining from the singer's eyes as he experiences the presence of his loved one.

Alison Reynolds- The Back Cover

Finally, there is the beautiful song excerpted on the back cover. Back to You was written by Alison Reynolds and in performance features three Las Cruces musicians: Paul Walter Kimball; Tim McKellar; and, Dave Ferris. The song is arguably a love song where she has wandered off somewhere, gotten a bit lost, and is now finding her way back to the person she loves.

But in her words, We see our own journeys. We find our own sense of wonder in her lines:

Don't understand
What it was that made me leave.
Don't know if I ever will

We often wonder at the state of ourselves, how did we get here, how did we leave "ourselves" and become something "not ourselves."

This old road goes on for
Miles and miles
Seems like it will never end

"This old road" certainly seems like the struggle so many of us face daily. Sometimes minute by minute, second by second. And the symptoms, the nightmares, the panic attacks, all seem like they are indeed a never-ending story.

Back to You

I'm on the road to somewhere
Where I'm bound I can't tell
I see your face so clear before me
Like an ever-present dream

It's been so long
Since I've made love to you
I want to hold you in my arms
It's been so long
Since I've gazed into your eyes
And seen the laughter shining through.

This old road goes on for
Miles and miles
Seems like it will never end

*I know there's one thing that I've
Got to do
Turn around and make my
Way back to you 'cause it's
It's been so long
Since I've made love to you
I want to hold you in my arms
It's been so long
Since I've gazed into your eyes
And seen the laughter shining through.*

*Well I
Don't understand
What it was that made me leave.
Don't know if I ever will
All I know is that I
Love you
And I'll be back this time
To stay*

*Now I'm on the road to somewhere
Where I'm bound is to you
I see your face so clear before me
And I can almost touch your
Hand*

*Oh it's
It's been too long
Since I've made love to you
I've got to hold you in my arms
It's been too long
Since I've gazed into your eyes
And seen the laughter shining through.*

But the parallels to Our journeys are only part of the reason. The other is far more personal, far more intimate.

When I first wrote to Alison, I felt I needed to tell her why that song was so important to me, to the book. There's something I do, and I have done this over and over: when I'm working on a project, there's always one song or one album that I will put on continuous play while I'm writing. The rhythm creates a comfort zone, kind of a song cocoon. This time, it wasn't simply a matter of cranking text, or code. It was a journey into the nexus of historical points – seeing how I didn't want to talk about how difficult it was to re-experience the Events that needed to be told. This is a part of what I wrote.

> *I'm a bassplayer. Rhythm for me is everything. And the percussion on that song is what's making it possible for me to make it through this. Sometimes exploring all the feelings is really hard and I need to know where the ground is.*

So when I was meandering through the morass, I was also holding on to that percussion line. Sometimes working more on figuring out how to do the turn pattern that he has 10 fingers to make and I have only my humble little pick. The challenge gave me a place to return home to. A place to be grounded in.

As you read the poems and songs in this book, reflect on the depth of emotion, of feelings, they reveal. Consider the strength of will that it has taken people to find their creative path, and to follow it. It's not a trivial exercise, although after all this time and with the help of each other, We make it through. Sometimes, it's days or even weeks We are good. Other times, it's a second-by-second struggle.

Clarity

Anyone who's hurt
When you're being who you are
Doesn't love you
Show me who you are
Let me learn what you need
I will love you forever.

Who am I

Who Am I – With You?, written September 12th, 2023, is a love story with a distinctly different point of view. It's also a stack of layers of feelings, of questions, of new ways of being. It's talking about how many things have changed, about the confusion and struggle to understand who they have become and then how and why they might have become it.

If You Aren't

If you aren't ready for
love then how can you
be ready for life?

(Aly, journal)

Introduced by Aly's *If You Aren't*, the two pieces complement each other, creating two different spaces for those existential questions: Who Am I? Frequently, the question is uttered in isolation, the desperate soul looking for relief. Here, the writers look outside themselves, to their relationships, their connections with others, and ask: *What world do we make together?*

Who am I – with you?

Who am I - with you?
I know what we've done
I know what we've said
But so many people have passed through that lens –
And now, it's just us, together
Soft, sweet – touching - tender
Who Am I? Who Am I?
Who is this person I don't know
The way I am with you is unfamiliar
Unfamiliar ways of feeling –
Soft, gentle, no defenses, no fear
Who is this person?
I have written this over and over different ways
Who Am I?...With you.

The small details are what really matter in a relationship

6: It's a kind of PTSD Magic

Because I'm missing you
Because I'm missing you
Everything goes away
With you

I'm missing
Missing you
Missing you

When you leave

You take it all away
You are the bedrock
For my soul
You are, just you
What keeps me whole.

I hear birds
For the very first time

But only because
They went away
With everything else
It all just went away
With you
And I'm so missing you.
I'm missing you
Just missing you.

In the lovely *Because I'm Missing You* that opens this chapter, the author shows both the wish for the missing one to be there and the underlying joy that is so present in the relationship you could almost feel it come through the pages and wrap you in it.

It doesn't matter who wrote it or who is who in the lyrics. It could go any way. And so many of the selections in this gentle tome show the delicacy, the precision, the love with which men can write.

This chapter is about having a working experience with the "vocabulary." Here, "vocabulary" does not mean the word you see as it might be written. Here, "vocabulary" means the myriad expressions of Events.

In Randy Lynch's hauntingly beautiful break-up songs, if you listen, you feel beyond the mere surface characteristics of the words, the way they're written, how they sound alone, how they look on a page – to the Events he is sharing with you, with the world. Even though he's a secret metalhead, he says everything he writes comes out Country. With a few notable exceptions, every song Randy writes is about the break-up of his marriage. Randy writes from his heart, transforming his pain, his anguish, his guilt, into art, into music, into a generosity of love.

And this transformation, like Aly's untitled piece below, shows the kind of "PTSD Magic" that comes from Growth. One might ask, Does that mean you don't have it anymore?

No, It doesn't mean that at all but it's a perfectly reasonable question that also allows the hope behind it to shine. And it's a question that those of us who have learned to use the new skills would never hope for. For some of Us, Posttraumatic Growth is a transformation that is reflected in the gifts We create. It means that a number of Us have, by what appears to be simply personal strength, dogged determination, a will to live a happier, more fulfilling life, or just plain orneriness, developed ways to control Our challenges.

Also, We are not "broken" so much as We have re-formed ourselves into new kinds of beings, people with distinctly unique ways of seeing the world.

(Untitled) Aly, 12/20/2023

I'm learning how to love
How to be patient
Every step I take
I'm learning how to strive.
In these deep summer nights.
I look into your eyes
See a future that is constantly disguised.

But when will you decide
That enough is enough?

I know that we play by the same rules
But You decide that I am not tough

That is all a lie
I'm learning how to fly
Find that spark within my eyes

Oh, warm brown eyes glitter
As a New Mexico sunset in your rear-view mirror.

That shimmer makes things better,
Only if you believe in it.

It Really Is a Kind of PTSD Magic

Some people will never "recover" but truly, what recovery is, is different for each of us. And based on what I'm seeing, what I'm hearing, growth takes a combination of courage, determination and a full-on willingness to rebel. Interestingly enough, it also takes an absence or lessening of the impacts of cultural socialization.

You state a theme and then take it for a walk in the woods.

The research and medical communities tell Us We are broken, beyond help, having no future without them but admit also that they have few successes. Authors in the popular culture characterize Us so beautifully, usually in the guise of someone considered to be "perfectly normal," just with a stressful job, like 'police detective':

> ...when she pushed us away, I was certain I'd never see her alive again. <u>Since then, it's like I'm always out of breath. Always a step behind, a moment too slow.</u> Because I don't know what the next moment will bring.
> Stone & Rhodes 2023, p. 61

This reaction, the response, the Story, is so classic, and yet it's made out to be 'just another' – but accepted – part of the job. Dismissed. Made into something else by the power of Story.

And We are more than Story. We are, and perhaps critically importantly, more than the Stories We create to communicate. And still more importantly, more deeply than that, We can access the Emotions, the Feelings, and then fashion them into Story, in these cases, musical Stories, lyrics that will combine with notes and movement to carry a select few into the realm of total understanding, total experience.

People often use Emotions and Feelings interchangeably but in the grand scheme of cognition, they are two very different animals. Emotions are sensory responses, that is, responses to what the body perceives. They are also a very important kind of knowledge because the body remembers Events, responses, and the results of those responses. As musicians, we notice these subtleties because we access them every day. Sadly, I think, most people pay little attention to what their body is telling them, having been firmly entrenched in the idea that the Mind is required for all functions. For most people, the "brain" is a single, integrated unit.

Emotions are generally brief. Feelings, on the other hand, may last much longer, and for some of us, are stored as separate data points with the Event representation. This is a bit of a dicey concept here, because the re-experiencing of an Event with the physiological responses needs to be distinctly separated from "memories," which seem to be more cognitive than visceral.

Feelings are created when a person becomes conscious of the physical information, conscious of what the body is saying. And the making of Feelings combines psychological, and environmental factors, as well as the physical sensory perceptions. We "interpret" those Emotions, give them names, categorize them, make up Stories about them. This process is also called *elaboration*, because of the additional information added to the raw data.

Interestingly, when Feelings are elaborated when they occur, they become intricately connected to the Emotions and Story data. And since the initial data has been changed, there's no way to re-experience the Event the way it originally happened, that is, in its pure, undressed-up form. This is important because when the original data have been contaminated, they cannot be used for comparison with new data. And this is important because what appear to be "memories" are actually a combination of the Event, the Feelings, and the Story created at the time. It's the same difference as between raw movie footage and the finished production.

Emotions are Not Feelings

Because many of Us have such intense Emotional responses to things, We have tremendous opportunities to learn and at a very fast rate. Hypervigilance has been characterized as a "problem" but the fact remains that for some people, myself included, the "hypervigilance" that has been made into "the bad guy" by the medical and research communities, and by the media, is the very thing that has kept us safe and alive for a very long time. And in practice, observably for some of Us, allows Us to monitor a wide range of activities in real time.

This highly tuned awareness can detect danger in the environment that is not obvious to those who have not been in many different situations nor to those who have learned to disregard their body's communications. As the world has become more complicated, as densities of humanity increase, the opportunities for bad ends increases. Hypervigilance gives us an Edge, a resource, that We use to ensure Our own safety and that of others. Yes, sometimes We appear to be what the Trolls might want to call "jumpy." But it's also who We have become.

Emotions Are...?

I really loved Latin in high school, so I think it's wonderful that the word for a PTSD gift that I value so highly comes from Latin. The source of the word Emotions is a 2nd declension Latin verb, *emovere*, which can mean *movement* or *replacing*, depending on the context. Emotions are physical responses, moving among physical sensors and brain activity, choreographed to a nuanced interplay of sensations, and the interplay of what our Brain believes We are seeing, hearing, feeling, smelling at any given moment in time.

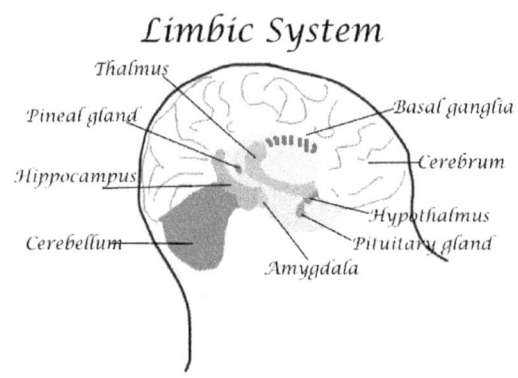

Emotions are a beautiful dance that blends outer and inner, takes a peek at history, moves the body to move or relax with little of what people call "thinking."

More than just words

In the research and medical communities, the Limbic System is often called the emotional brain. The entire Limbic System is composed of many different-sized parts, some small like the almond-shaped amygdala (light green) and some large like the Cerebellum (purple) and the Basal Ganglia (black). The amygdala and its functions are primary points of interest in PTSD research because it is heavily involved processing emotions like fear, pleasure, and aggression. The other cool thing it does is store emotional memories.

The prefrontal cortex, labelled *Cerebrum*, is intricately involved in the functional and social cultures that confront us. The prefrontal cortex, that part of the brain that aligns with our eyes and faces the world outside, is supposed to handle higher cognitive functions. Two important functions are regulating emotions and social behavior. Theoretically, the prefrontal cortex is supposed to provide the facility to modulate our feelings by letting us regulate emotional responses. But this assumes that our reaction time is slower than the time required for Emotions to become Feelings. While I can't prove it, not being a neurobiologist, I think that speed of responses, that is, how quickly neurons transmit their information, is a critical element in understanding how PTSD alters brain functioning. Simply put, if response times are shorter than the time it takes for machines to recognize and record the reaction, then they are just not seen at all: they are invisible.

The second thing the prefrontal cortex is thought to do is allow us to modulate our behaviors according to our socialization. This is an interesting point because many of us resist socialization and cultural norming. Especially for the Children of No Before, We know We are different but for a long time, We don't know how or why. It's only when We start talking with each other and sharing Our sensations – not Our thoughts or even Our Feelings – but Our Emotions and the physical sensations that tell Us what is about to happen – that We begin to understand *who* We have become.

The hippocampus makes our memories. It also offers up these memories when the opportunities arise and if this happens fast enough that impulses never have time to reach the thinking part of the Limbic System, the prefrontal cortex, We can be enjoying a meltdown of varying intensities or a panic attack, or a fast exit from where We were.

Along with the physical structures, there are what are called neurotransmitters that flood the brain with their special quality of chemicals that regulate our Emotions and resulting moods. These are pretty well-known and their names appear frequently in the popular press: dopamine, serotonin, and norepinephrine. ChatSmith says that neurotransmitters are *"messengers [that] help relay signals between nerve cells and can influence the intensity and duration of emotional states"* and it sounds so benign. What's really happening is that these liquids are flooding the brain and the more liquid, the more signals fire across the synapses, and the more chaos potentially ensues. This is the picture, the overall sense in real life, of what it feels like when that happens. (Retrieved 1/14/2024)

Research estimates put serotonin's first appearance 700-750 million years ago, predating dopamine and norepinephrine. And it's very common for living beings to increase their skills, tools, and resources as they go along. Neurotransmitters are no exception in this regard: "Not surprisingly, as a result of this long evolutionary history, serotonin plays a variety of roles in normal physiology, including developmental, cardiovascular, gastrointestinal, and endocrine function, sensory perception, behaviors such as aggression, appetite, sex, sleep, mood, cognition, and memory." (Nichols & Nichols, 2008). Basically, this means that serotonin has its fingers in all the pots and has been around long enough to develop some pretty sophisticated behaviors.

What doesn't show up in printed words is the movement they reference. The processing of Emotions and Feelings "is a dynamic and interconnected process that involves multiple brain regions working together in a highly coordinated manner." (Chat Smith, 1/15/2024). Neurons are sparking across gaps; neurotransmitters are flowing; impulses may be moving at the speed of light.

How Fast is Fast?

Actually, to us it can seem that way: Something happens; We react; We wonder what happened *after the fact*. The generally accepted speed of light is approximately 299,792,458 meters per second, while the speed of neurons ranges from a snail's pace 1 meter per second to almost muscle-car speed of 120 meters per second.

Here's where it gets really interesting. The fastest neurons are the motor neurons, with speeds of over 100 meters per second. If I were an Evolutionary Neurobiologist, I might hypothesize that this difference in speeds, not between neurons and light but between motor neurons and prefrontal cortex neurons at only 5-40 meters per second, proves that our ancestors didn't stop to think before deciding to run from the approaching carnivore.

On a related topic: I sometimes try to explain to someone how fast my body can react when it's responding to stressors. Now we know that speed to be more than 100 meters per second. And its communications can be causing numerous chemical reactions, messengers telling other parts of the body what to do. And meanwhile back at the ranch, the low-speed prefrontal cortex slumbers on.

In summary, the processing of feelings is a complex and multifaceted phenomenon that involves a network of brain regions working in concert to generate, interpret, and regulate emotional experiences. These processes are influenced by a combination of biological, psychological, and environmental factors, highlighting the intricate interplay between the brain, the mind, and the external world.

The James-Lange theory of emotions, proposed by psychologist William James and physiologist Carl Lange, suggests that emotions are a direct result of physiological responses to external stimuli. According to this theory, our emotional experience arises from bodily changes that occur in response to a stimulus.

This is my experience, that the emotions occur first as a physical response followed by a behavior that ranges across a spectrum of intensity. Sometimes, I am merely snarky; other times, and very rarely anymore, I feel like I'm being carried along by some force inside me that is "not me." I don't know what it is; I only know what it feels like.

There are other times when my emotional response is tempered by thinking about it. Examples are when one of my cats came home sick on the weekend, I had to temper my fear and worry to find veterinary care for her. When I spun out on black ice in the Cascades, I had to temper my fear in order to avoid something really bad happening, like careening over the edge into the river 400 feet below. So these and similar situations fit with the theory of cognitive assistance. We also need to remember that the instruments used to "measure" were developed by researchers looking to support their own theories. Additionally, experiments are complicated to set up, and so generally only one main idea will be investigated. This gives the impression, when cited by others, that the tiny slice is a "real thing" when actually it's simply a sliver of the bigger picture.

Making Connections

That connection with the few who can hear, who can see, who can 'be' with Us is critical to our lives. When I am PTSDing, which means I'm coping with a whole bunch of Feelings and Stories, edging down into darkness, when I feel the pain rise as a gasp, when the tears begin to flow in scrunched up face, when the isolation looms, beckoning comfortingly, when hope disappears into madness, when I'm listening to Dwight, the music of my escape, I send a message to my friends. It's simple: I'm in trouble. And people come, like We are there for each other. It's humbling to be so loved, so connected. I would ask, Why me? Now I know, from the joy I see in their faces, from the very fact that We are all here.

In general, We don't show Feelings. It's already automatic, so fast it's almost autonomic. Never show what you're really feeling; it could get you killed, or at least, badly hurt.

What's the Magic?

The magic begins to happen when We grasp the White Dragon by the neck, look it in the eye, and prepare to mount. Fanciful, perhaps, but the White Dragon symbolizes many things to many cultures. And the Story here is that PTSD and c-PTSD are Our bodies' reactions to the trauma, to the pain they endured. People in general bundle their Feelings, the ones that emerge after basic safety has been handled subconsciously, with their historical experiences together with the Stories they have told before to create a new Fiction.

Sometimes it is a "convenient Fiction:" being successful and having PTSD is a paradox. Sometimes it's a more well-thought-out Fiction: she's a star so of course she has all those people to help and I don't. The truth is, she's a star *because* she learned to manage.

The White Dragon: A Gentle Fiction

The dual nature of the White Dragon is appropriate as a symbol of the complex nature of PTSD: Powerful, pure, seemingly desirable in one guise, dangerous, ferocious but also powerful in the other. While I don't see dragons as particularly pure – after all, according to Anne McCaffrey, they live in weyrs, like barns, and I would imagine they get a little dirty out there. But that said, removing all the decoration, in both guises, dragons, like PTSD, are powerful.

And to mount your White Dragon is to know it: its scales beneath your knees; its pounding heartbeat; the smell of its breath; the gleam in its eyes. Still fanciful but metaphorically accurate. And hence The Magic.

Because PTSD is so multifaceted, rewards and treats accrue to those bold enough to take its measures. This isn't a how-to book; it's an Idea book that's specifically designed to show Ourselves to others who are like Us. So how one socializes one's White Dragon is a matter of personal growth and development. Every individual's growth story is different. In the beginning, everyone has the same goal: to take steps, make movements, change thinking, as methods of mitigation. To be able to live a somewhat peaceful existence with a different way of thinking that only a few understand.

I often find that when something has a name, it is far less scary. So We name Our differences. We know what We've got. Or better: how We changed because of not only the precipitating Event, but of how We are using the special extras to have fun in life.

> Marianne nodded sagely and said, in her low, soothing voice, "Talk therapy only goes so far. Trauma lives in the body. And the body's the only thing that can work it out."
>
> (Kirkland, 2023)

Research and the medical community like to list our "comorbidities" (such an awful word, I feel). These are anxiety; depression; flashbacks; et cetera. You've all heard it, read it. They don't talk much about the skills that also come: a fuller, more comprehensive range of Emotions as well as increased dynamics; synaesthesia; a powerful drive to succeed; complex and sophisticated empathy. These skills are common in my community. I would say they are only revealed and discussed in Our own company. And since researchers don't know they exist, they are unlikely to look for them. Further, their limited physical experience will limit their understanding. An additional fillip, like a fly in the ointment, would be the incredible difficulty of designing a research methodology to test the probability of these pretty much evanescent cognitive skills.

How Did It Get So Bad?

Besieged and beleaguered by the mass movement toward Skinner's belligerent Behaviorism in the 1930's, Research turned away from what was then both the current and the predominant theory that "physiological and behavioral responses precede subjective experience in emotions that are marked by distinct bodily expression." (Friedman, 2010). This is supported further by the simple consideration of processing speed: motor neurons for movement, for running away, for entering the fray, are two and a half to 20 times faster than those in the "thinking" prefrontal cortex. And it also means that as early as 1894, William James was aware that many decisions were made by people's bodies long, often very long, before physically higher cognitive resources were aware that an Event was taking place. And this is significant.

It means that those people who tell us that We can stop Events with our Minds are simply wrong. We can certainly change the Story after the fact, but the Body processes its sensations much, much faster than neurons can communicate with the cerebral cortex.

An essential element in brain research is speed: how fast does a research device like MRI or fMRI have to gather data to present a complete picture of what characterizes an Event? If communications to different parts of the brain happen faster than the tools can see and record them, then the subsequent analysis produces wrong results. Some will argue that the results are just "incomplete" and this is accurate, but it is not a simple matter, not an "it's just…" matter. Having all the details of what the brain does is essential to understanding the complex whole story, rather than presenting rich opportunities for speculation based on gaps in the picture.

Inside Out

The glorious part of PTSD that's called *posttraumatic growth* gives us skills that all we musicians seem to possess so I'm guessing many others have it too. It's the ability to play with people one way or the other.

There is only "one word" to understand here that is made for the blending of each idea, each implication, each shared understanding. Shared understandings on so many levels: lovers, Us, Not-Us, complex intersections where they meet and cross…meet and don't cross…meet and run together. So many possibilities in the spaces between.

And because We are so well stocked with rich resources and understandings in Our heads, We see things, do things, experience things that others who are Not-Us are not aware of. So that's Us, and Not-Us. And then there's the area in the middle, the gradient between where the quasi cases live. Where events cause temporary responses and where others' events cause traumatic responses.

This "In-betweenness" is not discussed in the literature, beyond recognizing that there are so many dimensions to PTSD they are having a hard time getting their heads and their pre-made, hypothetically driven "Indexes" around it. These "indexes" [Priebe, 2018] are questionnaires that allow them to add up the counts of each answer to each of the questions, run some groovy statistics, and then make a proclamation.

Now personally, I am very fond of "groovy statistics." What I am not a fan of is when the elegant voice of that elegant lady is forced to make people "less than" in the eyes of others. Not nice.

Research Profile

The research actually seems to divide into two basic groups: questionnaires, and meta-analyses. Meta-analyses are those where researchers, grad students, mostly, collect "results data" from other published reports, add it all together, run more groovy statistics, and make more groovy proclamations, usually with the end goal of getting more research money. Sometimes it's just a liner on their resume, preparation for their tenure bid. Sometimes it's a vehicle to give one or more grad students a leg up. The bottom line of all this analysis of possible motivation is that questionnaires and meta-analyses don't do anything to help the people they are using for research.

It might be a little extreme to compare the general state of research into PTSD with Tuskegee, but in fact IRBs should place more emphasis on how exactly "participants," that's what people who "do stuff" in research experiments are called, how exactly these people are helped by giving the researchers a leg up.

Another serious consideration about the research is that it has been done with graduate student volunteers. This is what's referred to as a "convenience sample," or in the vernacular, low hanging fruit. Students are easily accessible and are often given useful incentives to participate. They also do not have the inconvenience of being a "sensitive population." This would require a lot more additional work because of the special protocols and approvals required.

Current Theory

The current theory is that when we encounter a stimulus, our bodies automatically respond with physiological changes, such as increased heart rate, sweating, or changes in muscle tension. Research makes a leap here and believes that our bodily reactions then inform our subjective experience of emotion.

In other words, according to the James-Lange theory, we experience emotions based on our interpretation of the bodily changes that occur in response to a specific stimulus. For example, instead of feeling afraid because we perceive a threat, the theory proposes that we perceive a threat because our body responds with fear-related physiological changes. Uh-huh. Imagine the first time you bolted in fear. Did you say, Oh, those were fear-related physiological changes; I must feel fear. I think not. But who am I, you know? I mean besides someone who has lived with this since toddlerhood and has spent many hours exploring how all this works. But like I said...

However, it is worth noting that the James-Lange theory of emotions has been criticized, which is not unusual in fields where people cannot see what they are trying to understand. People want safety; they want security. They do not want to face the possibility that they might be wrong. Other people have proposed different theories. But no one anywhere, at least not that I have seen, has said, I have PTSD and this is my intuition about it. Instead we have people looking safely at it from shore, telling us how high the waves were, how many surfers died, and how many swimmers were rescued by dolphins.

So they argue about who's dog is doing what to that other dog. They have emotions involving physiological responses and cognitive processes together, but they aren't specific about where in the complex architecture of the brain these "cognitive processes" are happening.

I have a theory about brain speed and it's based on how fast the electrical impulses travel up the axons, the neurons' connecting structures. Motor neurons in my legs communicate at more than 100 meters per second. Neurons in the prefrontal cortex, which is also a long way away from my legs, communicate at between two-fifths (40/100) and $1/20^{th}$ of that speed: between 5 and 40 meters per second.

Many of the skills that kept us alive when we were just becoming humans are still highly functional today. The rods in the eye have a complex structure that allows them to rapidly and accurately determine the nature of movement and send determination information to the legs and feet. The message is simple: Dinosaur approaching. Get the hell out of Dodge.

Of course, there was no hell and there was no Dodge but you get the idea. The immediate response complex is a survival trait because subtle changes in the dappling of sun on leaves, the changes in the sounds of birds and insects, could indicate a predator. Pre-people who stopped to have a conversation to explore the possibilities probably aren't with us anymore. In these situations, bodies that react without spending time debating the options live while the more socially inclusive individuals have already become lunch.

Back when I knew less, I was always suspicious of people who chose careers or research interests based on events in their lives. Now, looking out from here on the inside, I see that meanings are often derived from your point of view, that one person can voice different meanings as they change their self-relative point of view and also their Context.

Context is really important because it describes where you are geographically, down so many levels, from the sky to the chair. It has the People, individuals and their nuances. This means that the possibilities of what Music emerges includes voices, spoken word, like Derrida first proposed, as well as instrumentals. Somehow, people got lost in the larger concept.

A Wander to Finish the Magic

I think I must be my own special kind of "adrenaline junkie." I don't particularly like adrenaline; I especially don't like epinephrine, because they make me light-headed and blurry, kind of. Strange, thin like transparent, but not *transparent*. Thin. So what kind of "junkie" do I have to be to *always* be on the Bleeding Edge?

This is what I will often call a "toy." It offers so many "dimensional possibilities." It's a simple concept, really, and it says that if you follow a particular idea, there are many different other ideas that seem to "connect" to it. You might be thinking about your upcoming family reunion and you remember a whiff of your grandmother's perfume. This takes you back to the summer you and the black-and-white pinto pony learned to ride together. Left undisturbed, this process can go on for a very long time, one idea leading to the next. The "connections" are called Associations.

I was walking into my friend Tim's workplace on one particularly New Mexican blowey day. I commented on it and Tim began to whistle. I said, Did you really make that association?

The missing linear piece of data is that Tim was whistling *Windy*, released in 1967 by The Association, a band out of California. The album was Insight Out.

So truth be told, We aren't really "unfocused" nor do We necessarily have "trouble" focusing. Several of us agree that We have no trouble whatsoever focusing on things We are really interested in. We do, however, have "trouble" focusing on things We don't want to do, things We find boring. We have no trouble focusing on the magic that is us.

A friend and I were walking past a small pond in Florida after lunch. We stopped to enjoy the shade, the water plants. I said, *Oooo, look at the fish! Aren't they gorgeous.*

She looked at me blankly: *What fish?*

There, beneath the surface.

She didn't know how to see beneath the surface of the water. It was interesting teaching her and she was so happy she had learned a new way to see. At least, with ponds. I doubt she applied this methodology to other areas of her visual opportunities, but who knows?

My friends and I are gifted with the ability to see beneath the surface. Oftentimes, it's because We have spent so much time really getting to know what's happening inside us that We can see multiple levels beneath the surface.

A skill that We have built using this gift is Our perception of the humor in what are otherwise horrifying situations. As We peruse the levels, and explore the details, the Feelings, We can decide that their terribleness is just too much trouble, too much "been there, done that, have the t-shirt in the closet."

As We cascade down, the humor increases until We can create the most absolutely funny, usually black-humored expression of what has now been transformed into a minor aggravation. On the downside, ordinary people who do not experience the full range of emotions possible in any given situation, look at us funny. They think we are cray-cray. They don't know it's Them.

But that is an interesting correlation right there. The Cray was at one time the most sought-after beast in computing history. Water-cooled, the brainchild of Seymour Cray, first released in 1976, it was the forerunner of today's supercomputers. And the descriptions of its key features are perfect comparisons for how many of Our Brains work.

Of course, the sample population, my friends, is not particularly diverse. We are musicians. That's all. No Age, Gender, Race, Color, Creed, because unlike certain genetically related diseases, for example, Cystic Fibrosis; Huntington's Disease; Sickle Cell Anemia; Down Syndrome; Hemophilia; Muscular

Dystrophy, (Adapted from ChatGPT, November 8th, 2023), PTSD does not reach out to anyone in particular.

People have searched for genetic links (Broekman, et al. 2007), not because there are any, but because it's easy to get grant money for basic research. It's part of the common hope-transformed-into-desperate-belief that every cognitive challenge can be "cured" by a pill, a shot, something medical, preferably with an "instant cure" characteristic.

Realities and Stories

But every Reality is a Story. It's the Story you write, but it's also the Story They write. The Story of Everyone's response to emotions, feelings, mood, was first planted in Aristotle's time according to researchers who opened their story of Neural Pathways with this compelling statement:

"Through the centuries, great philosophers (Plato, Aristotle, Spinoza, Descartes), doctors (Aristotle and Galen), neurophysiologists (Broca, Papez and McLean), neuropsychologists, neurologists, psychiatrists etc., [essentially everyone] have considered emotions to be mysterious and irrational experiences..." (Stanislovik, et al., 2023, p. 1)

"...mysterious and irrational experiences..." This pretty much tells you about the context for cognitive understanding that was established 2,000 years ago. Nothing has really changed from then.

7: Soundscapes of Our Lives

It's a lonely world when you can't make connections. When you can't find a happy juncture to share a laugh; nod to the identical ways you do things; react to things; respond to things. It's a lonely, lonely world when you can't share your joys and pains with someone who understands, with someone who needs no explanations, asks no intrusive questions that will throw you off the path of your story. Because everything we are is Story; our lives are one long Story with interconnected Events. We tell them as carefully constructed stories, design the words, design the sounds, design the images the songscape of Story will emotionally, physically, evoke.

A telling to a friend

[it starts]
You seemed so proud.
[zoom]
Your hand holds mine
                      I'm crashing
                          Falling
                          Going down
                      The flames were up
                      Around
                    I've spent another song
                            with him

> *He's not dead*
> *Oh yes. He is.*
> *The Little Mess drives home.*
> *The tears don't quench the flames*

[burn]

It's who We are, and We offer forward a complete picture of who We are, everything in balance according to where We are at the moment. It's not a picture of perfection by any standards but Ours where it precisely and accurately represents who and how We are at the moment We are telling the Story.

> We can't "tell" about It, but we can write and let who and how we are share what It is in a way that could never be captured by Story.

The True Nature of Story

But as convincing as this argument is, and I believed it myself for a good long time, until I was working one day with another songwriter and we were talking about how we processed. We realized that long, long before there is "story," there are the physical responses to what's happening in our bodies. And we also noticed that it took time for those responses to become communicable. Sometimes, it took a long time for it to reach our heads, to become words, to be ordered into Story. And sometimes, it just never did.

And with that attention to the detail of process, in slow motion, we realized that Story is not all we are. Story is all We are to those who see only our outside. And as musicians, our outsides are more often than not performances. This is what We do; this is our art, our souls on display. But even so, there are many layers between soul and the skilled, practiced performance.

> You kinda notice when you start thinking in guitar

> (December 17th, 2023)

> Or when the music of a rant is a blues riff

> (January 21st, 2024)

These kinds of artistic transformations can be really scary and often inscrutable to non-Musicians. They might well wonder, How do they do that? How can those people who we think are so "broken" they can't possibly do anything big, anything impressive, anything gentle, determined, humanistic? In short, How can those people whom we have written off be standing so tall and strong, and in a space we can never enter?

Beyond Perceived Limitations

One attitude that characterizes each of the Musicians here is a dogged determination to succeed, to reach beyond the perceived limitations to the abilities that We have because of traumatic and life-changing Events.

These chapters share the sounds, words and feelings of the musicians who have created them. They are all my friends. They all volunteered into the creation of this book. They have all coped with loss and struggle in some way. Sometimes, as musicians, we write not so much for ourselves as for others, for others to know, to feel, to see new vistas – or old ones in different ways.

In Chapter 5 we talked about the many uses of Edges, the many ways they can be defined, and importantly, why Edges tell the careful observer when We have maxed out Our comfort level. Edges are songs; they have messages that are meant to be understood.

As people we are never more vulnerable than when we are crafting the Music of Love. But the Music gives us a whole different language AND ways to say intimate things that we wouldn't be able to say face-to-face. Many of us are introverts and introspectives. The introspection gives us up-close and personal experiences with Our Emotions and Feelings. Introversion makes it less likely that We will share the beautiful understandings We have crafted in Our conversations with Our own Minds. But Music lets Us put all of these together in ways that We can share.

And I know I often wonder, What is it like for others? What do you feel when you anticipate seeing me? Holding me? Taking me to your secret place, to your heart?

And along with a sharing of the experience, the songs contain an exuberance, nuances of new growth, sometimes so subtle as to be unnoticeable, other times dramatic and attention-grabbing.

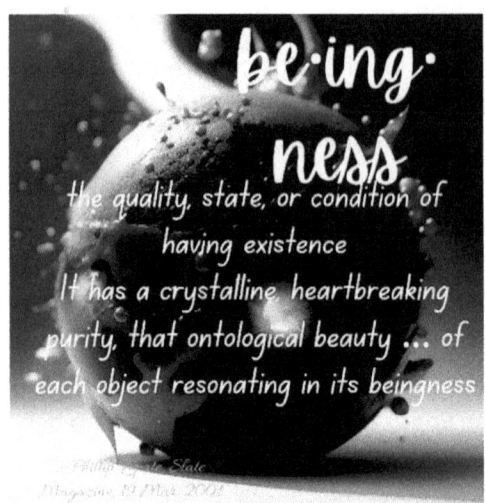

8: The Sound Walk

In the Beginning, All Was Vibration ...

Laura Bressan

What is sound? According to modern science, it's vibration. If you examine the core of an atom, you will realize that all matter is One. This conclusion is derived from nuclear science and Einstein's concept of "All is Energy."

The entire universe, what you can see and what you cannot see, is One flow of Energy; everything is manifested through an electromagnetic flow.

In the ancient Indian text "The Vedas" it is written: at the beginning all was vibration. The Vedas are the sound manifestations of the breath of life.

Considering now what we call human beings and all that we can see and perceive in this world. What defines human health and feelings?

The human mind can and in fact creates our own life experience. This can be an unconscious process or a conscious one. The mind can go astray to any length, but it can also break free from all control and limits, creating from the Source within us all: The One Truth, the individual fundamental vibration every being carries within themselves in this reality.

Science tells us that there are sounds outside the human auditory spectrum in the same way that there is light that does not pass through the lens of human eye.

When we listen to a musician singing on the radio, the sound of their music is converted into electromagnetic waves which travel through space. But how do we hear the music? We do convert them into sound waves.

Everything we need is within us. We do create our experience.

All is Energy, All is Vibration, flowing, accelerating in a Cosmic Movement of Expansion.

All is One and One is All. I do Exist therefore I am One, I am All.

Vibration is the coming downward of the One Energy that all is and all embrace, expanding unconditionally and without end. Everything we see, we hear, we experience is a manifestation of this One Truth whose only desire is to expand, to grow.

Vibration is the exact same One Energy but bending, varying, taking forms and creating in order to expand. We have infinite vibrations in the vast universe and they represent the infinite possibilities of everything that already exists and can or cannot take form depending on resonance.

So Vibration is like an individuation of the One Energy. And it's the only way everything takes form.

So, What is Actually a Sound?

A sound results when the One magnetic energy field is transformed into different realms of perception. The human realm of perception is just one of many, as science has confirmed that, like for light, there is an infinite range of sounds that cannot be perceived by human ears.

But have we not just said that everything is One Energy? So, what is a human then?

A human is an individuation of the One Energy through many layers that interconnect and align manifesting what we see as human body. The essence of a human in fact is not human at all. We are all One, we are all the same. We are entangled, there are no boundaries, no limits.

These are my current beliefs, beliefs that I feel deeply embodied in me in this life that I am consciously experiencing right now. But like for everything, mine was a journey; a great adventure indeed, that lead me to embrace the real nature of Who I am, What I am and How I can serve the supreme good: Never-ending Expansion, that is.

My Journey To My Voice And Sound Healing

I was born in Italy in a hospital in a village in the Verona district in 1987.

Ever since I can humanly remember my childhood, I have always experienced different consciousness states and different realms first-hand.

I clearly remember when I was about six years old and I ended up at the hospital after eating an entire chocolate Easter egg all by myself. During that night, I told my mother how beautiful the coloured rainbow spirals coming from above were and asked why I could not catch them with my human hands.

You can imagine the response of my mother at that time. It is perhaps normal for a child to have an invisible friend when they are little but this was the first time she understood I was seeing things beyond the dense human radar.

Everyone was so worried about my health. They thought I had some unique illness or worse, that I could have a brain tumour, so I spent a few days at the hospital doing all sorts of tests.

Of course, nothing was wrong with my health, I was simply seeing the energy. Something that is still embodied in me today.

In my family nobody was open to this world so I ended up not sharing my experiences with anyone; not wanting to look weird and gain unnecessary attention. But this became more and more of a challenge while I was growing up and my senses were more and more open.

My first approach to singing was thanks to the church. I was part of my local church choir; I had joined it because everyone thought I had a beautiful voice and I was always singing by myself but like everything in my life, I tend not to fit in. I have to create my own space, my own experience. This is a leitmotif of this conscious experience that is my life as Laura Bressan.

After a while I left the choir, and I started ballet where I found a way of creating my own space and I stayed in contact with my creative self for many years.

At 14, I fell in love as deeply as I could have. I left everything that I was doing behind and threw myself into a whole new world. It was a carefree time for me but I was already reminded of what a cycle is and what means to go astray from your own fundamental vibration and not being able to let go the known for the unknown.

That same year a dear friend of mine left their human body, it was a long trying battle, the one they fought. They left their physical body the late evening of September 10th; the day after, together with this, I watched the twin towers collapsing on TV. I remember feeling speechless.

I felt something big was changing inside me but I did not have the level of awareness I have right now. And I did not catch the communication that life was trying to bounce back at me.

A few years later I remember my grandma also left her physical body on September 11th. Angelina ("little angel" in English) is my grandma's name. She used to sing when she was little. I found out about this years after her departure from the physical realm in this version of my life. She wanted to sing but she could not. Her family was very poor and she had to work in agriculture all of her life.

Years later, I was shown that my Voice gift is coming from her. When I was shown this in a consciousness journey I did, I was still battling with the attachments of a romantic belief of what is the Truth about life. Because in Reality when I say that everything is One Energy, this means that the deeper we travel into the intangible, the more we deconstruct what is the manifested image of this world, and the more we realise that there is no Laura, there is no Angelina, there is no mother and father. There is in fact nothing of the sort. Energy is all that exists and everyone represents one of the infinite versions of the infinite unique modes of experiencing the expansion. That's beyond any human imagination.

In my childhood, then teenage and university years, I collected a variety of what you would call extra sensorial experiences. This made me believe the intangible layers of life are in fact Very Real and linked to everyone's consciousness frequency. We just need to be open to the possibility of catching the moment, feeling the moment. Because what is life, if not a perception of your own beliefs?

My Sound Creation Process

While I started venturing into different courses from a spiritual perspective, I had already started studying the Voice. I tried three teachers and I stopped looking after meeting teacher number three: Mrs. Alessandra De Negri.

Affectionately called "maestra" ("teacher" in Italian) Alessandra is an Italian soprano opera singer who is very connected to her fundamental vibration and believes in what I would call the process of creating your own sound. I was taught for over 12 years opera voice techniques for modern singing, while developing my own sound creation process. Creating the Sound from within your own vibrational wave was the key that unlocked everything for me.

She always encouraged me to do the impossible. During our one-to-one sessions, on top of technique the focus was always on the feeling inside me when developing a sound. How I felt in my physical body, how I felt emotionally, how I saw the sound, how the sound spoke to me.

I was once told that I do have an excess of energy that I feel the need to share with my "outside world." I was told multiple times that my talent was my Voice as well as that my guide would appear when the time was right. And that I was not in need of any course or anything similar to fulfil my spiritual and vocal path.

I have always been connected to my voice, to the music, to singing. But there was a time when I closed myself in a closet and tried hard to fit into what society wanted.

Alongside my passion for singing and my extra sensorial abilities, I always nurtured a deep desire to share my happiness and somehow support others in their development. This is how I ended up having a career in Human Resources for over 10 years after leaving my music career before it could really take off.

My office career led me to live in different countries, meet many people, travel the world, all of it without losing the creative space in my heart. This because everything I did was from the heart and with passion that I succeeded.

In 2019, after months of tests between the UK and Italy, I was diagnosed with endometriosis. I had lost mobility and could not really walk properly anymore. This was a trigger for me to think of what I really wanted to do in my life. I got the opportunity to self-reflect and gain insights from my heart.

Over what I would then recognise as the last years of my corporate career life, my desire to be more truthful to myself and do something in life that really reflected my talents was growing bigger and bigger.

But what were my talents?

The Voice? Music? Extra sensorial abilities?

I really love feeling connected to my Core and I thought I had already explored my music career when younger. I also felt I was too old to start again in the music industry.

So, a period of looking outside what I already had inside began.

I got certified in Reiki Usui II level; I became a Ho'oponopono practitioner. I learned about birth charts and evolutional astrology. I became a Shinrin Yoku facilitator; I practiced Shamanic Journeying and shamanic chanting and healing. I became an Imaginal Regression and Progression Operator. I worked with family constellations and mandalas, soul retrieval journeys; I did medicine wheels; met shamans in the Philippines and Australia; and had many more experiences.

By 2021 I was hitting my own belief ceiling. I had learned so much and yet I was feeling something was not right. I knew I needed to leave my job behind but was too scared to do it and did not want to hear that what I needed was just my Voice.

Realisation sometimes needs to travel your way through hardships. So, I fell ill, and like other times in my life, nobody could tell me what was wrong with me. I stayed in the hospital and on sick leave for a little while and towards the end of 2021 I realised it was all due to me not being aligned with my fundamental vibration: I quit my job and started everything from scratch.

It is at this point that, through a colleague of one of my holistic masters, I got to connected with the Maestr'ale Association and I felt like I was finally coming home. All those years of refusing to accept the Truth that was always within me, all the pieces of the puzzle came together at once.

It is at this moment that I clearly saw and accepted that My Voice is the only way for me to experiment with this life of which I am consciously aware, at its highest level.

To use the Voice it's my fundamental vibration calling me, and now that I fully understood and could hear the call to action from my system, I had to go back to My Voice and Music.

Through the Maestr'ale Association I got the opportunity to work on my fundamental vibration expansion journey and to reach a state that I would call active neutrality while I started again studying and practicing the Voice, this time around specialising in jazz vocals and studying pianoforte while perfecting my emptiness and silence for channeling the Source within me.

At this point I had left every holistic practice I was doing before my illness in 2021 to pursue my voice and music and after two years I have become a singer songwriter.

In 2022, always through the Maestr'ale Association, I then met my current Reiki Master Giancarlo Serra who facilitates Reiki and other healing techniques across the globe moving mainly between Sardinia (Italy) and London (UK). I started practising Reiki again from a completely new perspective, the non-dual approach, and I took the II level of Holy Fire Reiki.

At this point in my journey, it is clear to me that healing means re-aligning the system to the unique fundamental vibration frequency.

Nothing in this world comes to harm me. Instead, everything represents the infinite part of my non-tangible self speaking to me. Nothing is an exception to this, not even emotions and thoughts. Everything is a reflection of my inner core vibrational state.

While working on my self-expansion and on my Voice and music, it became clear that my extra sensorial abilities can be married with my Voice. I was then guided to experiment and perfect what naturally happens to me while I share Reiki and any other holistic practice and/or technique.

My Personal Experience – The Sound Path

When I practice Reiki, Shamanic Journey or even when I compose music, what happens to me is like entering into a stream of consciousness.

Everything feels completely blending and I am not feeling human at all. I am not feeling any limits or any boundaries. It's liberating.

When I compose, I put my hands on the pianoforte and I let go. I have to press the record button on my digital workstation to be able to "recollect" what comes out from my hands and voice through a recording.

In these moments I am channeling my Source, my Inner Voice and sending to myself messages in form of music and lyrics.

It is something that I believe happens to every musician and artist/creator; maybe some are more conscious than others of what is really happening. But the fact remains. We do tap into an unknown and infinite universe of frequencies where we do download the one message that is resonating with our system the most in that moment. This way music and lyrics flow within the composer out onto the score sheet.

Nowadays the music business wants you to go back to the music, go back to the lyrics and make a beautiful package out of it for your audience. Something that is easy on the listener's ears. That has a pattern that can be recognised and will therefore attract people who are going to come back for more.

This is the framework: letting the composition flow out of you first and then crafting it.

It is very important for me when I am working on a song, that everything from the beginning to the end of the process, is actually tuned on my core. In my opinion, this is the only way a musician can reflect their own heart into their music. Changing a song for any input that is not your deep gut feeling or heart, it is deviating from your true self.

David Bowie once said that he doesn't make music based on any of his influences, that he doesn't even consider himself a musician. He doesn't want to fit into anything when he creates. Everything comes out as a form of self-expression and music is a tool for him.

I was watching one of his interviews just before writing this chapter for my friend and colleague AJ's book, and David Bowie was saying that an artist should never create to please anybody else, they should create for themselves.

Who are we trying to please or comply with anyway? Everything is One Energy. To create for somebody else is a misbelief and we musicians sometimes lie to ourselves trying to make it big by looking for anything we could do in order to get a result.

The same concept shall be applied to sound healing practice: To aim at a specific result is to limit our infinite possibilities of creation.

When I do share sound vibrational healing, Laura Bressan is completely wiped out from the moment. With this I mean that there are no filters pertaining to Laura's ego while I am fully and completely entrusted to the One Energy. I am the One Energy.

I would like to say something meaningful and explanatory at this point. Something that could clarify what actually happens between my dense bodies, the Source, the vibration, the sound frequencies and the healing itself but this would mean to negate the fundamental Truth: that All is One.

The only clarification I can give here is that in these moments I experience the Flow of Life and I am One with All.

There is always a moment before starting any session when I clear my thoughts and focus the intention on Being One with the person, I am having the session with, or with the group I am facilitating the session.

This I believe can enhance the focus of the practice. That's all.

It is also very important to say that I am not saving anyone nor healing anyone. Since we are all One Energy, I am simply feeling the message my higher self is sharing and I am facilitating blocks of energy or densities to start flowing again.

While practising a Voice sound healing, I feel One with everything. Like I said before, there are no limits, no boundaries. Everything really feels connected and I lose touch with what are the human delimitations of space, matter and time.

This is because the process transcends the three dimensions and taps into the part of ourselves where everything is everywhere and anytime. The feeling of immersing yourself in this state cannot be considered an emotion, but if we need to put a label on it somehow, I would say that is a state of consciousness where I experience everything, every moment all at once and I instinctively feel where to focus my Voice.

This is where the sound comes in. It could be a practice that emerges from silence or with an accompaniment tuned at a particular frequency like 432 Hz, the hearth frequency. It could also be done in conjunction with a Tibetan bells sound bath.

Whatever the starting point is, I let everything that is not my Core Voice go, I am in the moment, feeling present and fully entrusted to the One Energy that I am.

And here it comes, I start vocalising and making sounds reaching specific frequencies and feeling the direction I need to take with the particular person and/or the group of people I am with.

I do this also by myself. It feels completely freeing and uplifting aligning my Voice to my Fundamental Vibration just to be there.

While it could all seem that I am doing something to others, I am fully aware that the other person at a certain level is me because we are all connected. So, there is no desire to help or save anyone.

And it is especially because there is attachment to a specific result that the best outcome for everyone involved will manifest.

What is certain is that I support the flow by realigning the energy flow and reestablishing its stream. Then to heal or to cure whatever is that we feel we need to overcome is a matter of working on the communication that comes with whatever symptoms or life situations we are experiencing. But more importantly it is only welcoming what that particular situation tells me that I am going to produce a change in my outer mirror. So it is always a work on myself.

During the sessions I don't know what will happen, and I use my voice as my Core commands. I let go of any expectations. Sometimes it gets very chilly and sometimes it gets very warm, sometimes I feel goosebumps, sometimes I have visions, sometimes I hear words or messages. What is a common denominator is that I lose the sense of me being Laura, my arms and legs become numb and I move with the sound of my voice.

Sometimes I produce a chanting, sometimes I sing, sometimes I produce sounds that could not be heard by human ears or sounds that are not considered nice to hear.

When I am immersed in the practice, I have no choice but to follow the commands of my Core.

Reiki Master Giancarlo Serra is currently guiding me to fully embrace my voice healing journey so I am very glad to be able to speak about it in this book, this is also being very helpful for me. I put everything I am on the table and I discovered a few things about my beliefs and my go-to thoughts thanks to the writing process.

I am also not scared to say that today I am 36 years old and I am starting my life from scratch for the 5th time and it is exciting as well as terrifying. But to believe is everything!

So, I trust The Sound Path, my newborn healing voice project and in continuous development. I am creating a selection of voice healing sounds that are going to be available on Spotify and other major streaming platforms to share some Love sound frequencies focused on particular parts of the human dense system (physical, emotional and mental bodies).

I truly thank the author of this book for taking a leap of faith with me and asking me to collaborate on their creation with an entire chapter on Sound & Voice Healing.

And I am so thankful to everyone I encountered on the road so far. Every step was a learning curve and I am grateful that I have finally combined my voice and extra sensorial abilities. Now I know why it needed to be now and not earlier on.

Everything is ever changing, life is movement and if we want to truly live, we shall reflect the ever-changing nature of it ourselves.

9: Ageism & Other Biases

When you wave your age, you're saying: This is what you can expect from me. In other words, you are saying that you share a cultural expectation based on sociocultural norms. You simultaneously lock yourself in to multiple sets of behaviors, even commonly accepted ways of saying things.

You may use it because it seems so much in the common parlance that it almost *feels* wrong not to do it. It also seems that it is so ubiquitous – that means, everywhere you look – that it doesn't *seem* to have meaning or implication other than being a number.

But if you are constrained to your age group, even if you choose who you want to hang with, if you don't see yourself reflected, you won't be comfortable and you won't know the reason why.

Growing from traumatic experiences means trying a few more scary things. Therapists may call it "stepping out of your comfort zone." As an aside here for a sec, there are no "zones" painted on a floor somewhere; no zone labeled "comfort" in which you are to perceive yourself standing; and no place labeled "discomfort zone." And that's why it's just easier to say, Try some more scary things.

One thing about scary things is the time it takes to do them. Enter here a common teaching misconception: If I tell you this, then you've got it, right away and forever.

That's simply not true and common experience will bear that out for everyone. In the same way that learning takes time, repetition, and enough exploration to build enough context to ground the new knowledge, engaging scary things also takes time and exploration and repeated tries.

Ageism with its subconscious, embedded expectations, is one of the most socially accepted methods of increasing the discomfort of people coping with the aftereffects of trauma.

Common examples: "Oh that was good. You're a big girl now." "Typical 4-year-old behavior." Motown signed Stevie Wonder when he was 11; enjoyed his first #1 hit when he was 13: "making him the youngest artist ever to top the chart" (MPP Digital Team, 2020) The first example both conditions behavior and receives acceptance because of the child's desire to be an adult. The second reflects a perhaps subconscious stereotype of what children of a particular age should be, should be able to do. And this is clearly reflected in the last example that singles the singer out, not because of his accomplishment but because of his age.

Julia Penelope is a lesbian linguist who wrote a book about how language frames us, creates our identities in the minds and therefore eyes of the people who are "not us." This is an important detail, that often what the mind believes, the eyes see, the ears hear, the body feels. And then, other social conditioning, deeply embedded, automatically paints our behavioral responses.

Julia's book is called "Speaking Freely: Unlearning the Lies of the Fathers' Tongues." This is a special case here, because many would question my use of her first name in a semi-academic context. Actually, it's a segue to the little-known fact that Penelope is her middle name. Dropping her surname was a physical statement of what she was saying and what she was trying to say.

"What she was saying" was what was communicable in ordinary language. "What she was trying to say" encapsulates the message in her book: We have things to say and we don't have language to do it."

Writing this book is not so different, because the "father's language" that constrains us, defines us, tries to make us and everyone else believe we are the pictures, pictures at an academically defined exhibition. We are not.

So Julia's extensive work in how language norms, which result from group socialization, marginalize and restrict people. She has provided a detailed analysis of how the often subtle, sometimes ingeniously nuanced, dynamically emerging implications that reflect social and cultural secrets intersect with the dynamics of power and identity.

This book has challenged our "father's language," defining Us not by labels or epithets but by describing in the best way We can, Our Emotions and Our Experiences. Collapsing across sociocultural age barriers, limitations, restrictions, We have emerged in Our own often fragile, sometimes doddering, often intense way to say what "it" is for us.

My friend Chuck Sutherland posted this one day: *You are not Scottish because you were born there. You are Scottish because it was born in you.* This is a way of saying that what you have, what you are, who you are comes out.

You have to be willing to be really vulnerable to trust yourself enough to go directly from Emotions, that is, what your body is saying, Not to what your words are saying. (Conversation in Messenger with Charles Sutherland, 3/7/2024).

We find ourselves transformed in a way there are no models in the world for. We can't just look at the work that someone else has done. We have to build the models of Our understanding from within ourselves and by sharing with others like us. It's "a new you." My version of "a new you" allows my totally wikid humor to emerge as:

My mother might have thrown me out that window because she thought I was a witch and she wanted to know if I could fly.

What this recasting accomplishes is lifting the heaviness from the Story. Instead of presenting the stark reality head-on, it gives the listener or the reader a chance to explore the possibilities that this might be a joke, that it might be a total put-on. Only after they have tiptoed through their cognitive valley of tulipian options a la Tiny Tim are they face-to-face with the horrifying truths.

Sharing Crayons

Query to ChatGPT, 01/08/2024: *What do people with PTSD have in common with those who don't?*

People with and without PTSD share common human experiences, emotions, and basic needs. Both groups can feel joy, sadness, and fear. They seek connection, understanding, and a sense of purpose. While individuals with PTSD may have experienced trauma, it's essential to recognize our shared humanity and the potential for empathy and support.

In this ending, you can hear a recognition of the shared bias, the shared "ism." And note the difference in the responses when the comparison targets are reversed:

Query to ChatGPT, 01/08/2024: *What do people who don't have PTSD have in common with those who do?*

Both individuals with and without PTSD share the fundamental aspects of being human. They have similar needs for social connection, understanding, and emotional well-being. While experiences may differ, the commonality lies in the desire for a fulfilling life, relationships, and a sense of purpose.

See how different this is? More upbeat? Less sad, less depressing.

Chats with others who cope with the aftereffects of trauma present new dimensions to Our different perspectives. Recently:

"me, too. I don't have any problem staying focused on the total picture. Which is usually too big and nuanced and beautiful for the average, 8-crayon person.

"And besides, the story is not the story without the details in the edges."

"Details in the Edges" commonly take the form of what could be heard, viewed and subsequently labeled as "tangents." But another friend said, "All those stories are necessary for the overall story." This wasn't "consolation." This said that she, too, though in terms of what I can only describe as a collection of related bodily and cognitive "bubbles" that together make the complete Story.

For Us, there is a deep, underlying need for the "overall story," the complete Story. Because in truth what We are saying is, "Know Me. I know I am different. I know there are no words. Please try."

10: Is There Love After PTSD?

How do you know if somebody likes you? You know, I can never figure that out. I can think I know, but then I somehow screw up the physical response signals and the other person gets the wrong meaning and goes away. And most times, I'm just oblivious.

But Love, when you feel it with your Body, hurts. There is that feeling of gratefulness that rises from somewhere deep inside you. There is that want to push it down, push it away, because the emotions are unfamiliar. But they are deep, physical. You want to know what love is, but you don't. But you do. And then, you don't. And if you're brave, you do it anyway. This will be my first time on that level.

Emotions Aren't "Feelings"

There is a huge difference between *Emotions* and *Feelings*. Emotions are physical and occur before the upper brain, the cortex, processes them into meaning. However, the lower, older, more specialized parts of the brain receive the original inputs and decide whether a fight-or-flight plan is needed long before any logical, meaning-making process occurs (Damasio, 2004).

Is There Love After PTSD?

So you're in love; you wake up in the morning gloriously happy, loved one by your side. You gaze into each other's eyes with boundless love falling out around the edges. You anticipate the night – or often just a moment from now – when you will take each other in your arms. He will take you, slowly, firmly, letting every inch of your waiting love know he is there, with you, carrying you, high and higher, close and closer to him.

His love explodes within you, cascades of delicate color, over and over. You follow, tremulous with wonder, your love growing deeper ... and then maybe you "come to your senses," that awful part of you that to your creative mind, spoils the fun. It says, Why would you want to give up all the familiar pain and misery for this amazing joy, this amazing and unbelievable happiness... and for the first time in your life you gaze out with knowing, loving eyes and say, Because I can.

> So I'm sitting here, pondering, and I realize that I am the only person I know willing to take on PTSD and Change not only my Behavior, but also how I think, because I loved one man enough to want to be with him that much. *(Instagram message to Aly on October 9th, 2023.)*

This is a love story

I started out to shred the research community for taking such a distant, abstracted view of the richness that is PTSD and its derivations, derivatives and beautiful opportunities.

As I worked on it, the people around me emerged like --- *mushrooms* is wrong, but it's like being in a forest and one day the ground is flat but rich with the hummus of decaying leaves and then in the night the moisture comes and the next day mushrooms are there in sharp relief and they're all different these mushrooms but all the same because they're mushrooms. In my case, not mushrooms but musicians and we all have, well, let's just say we all have the same disposition. Umm, some people might call it a "mood" but you know, moods kind of come; they go; they're like clouds. Dispositions are just kind of like how you are over time. It's like climate as opposed to weather and if you don't know that you probably wanna look it up, umm. And then, something continued happening in a very in, in what for me was a strange, a strange experience. I would have these conversations with Liam in my head as I worked through questions in the book, as I worked through how things came together and where the music went. I saw his music, especially his trumpet solos, when I felt how I was creating chapter dynamics. I mean not all of these things certainly because a lot of it just flows through me. But at critical junctures, there would be these, these conversations that led to clarity. And that was a phenomenon I, I had never seen before.

It's unique and special. It was – it *is* – pretty amazing. So today, December 11th, 2023, I'm realizing that the last chapters of this book really need to be not a conclusion but a new beginning. Is there love after PTSD? and the answer is yes: this was, still is, Liam's and my love story: it's the music beneath the words. It's Lost in the Rhyme, where every word I write is a new song for you. Loving you is the adventure of a lifetime.

> *I started falling in love with him at the edge of his aura.*
>
> *And was gone by the endless time, a spin around the stars, to his heart.*

This is a unique and different love story because it doesn't end when they kiss. It goes on, following the things they do, always a reflection of how it is to be musicians with PTSD who are in love. It's a story of hope and beauty; a story of love and reflection. And it will go on forever…

12:43 Sunday October 15th

And when that tiny little girl
Put up her arms
For the people she loved
To come, to pick her up
To hold her, to tell her they loved her
No one came
And after countless times
Countless Emptinesses
The little girl realized
Or thought or felt
Whatever
That the people she loved
Would never want her
After all, she had proof.
The very people who should have proved that her idea was wrong
Didn't – And so. She never believed.

11: Connections & Community

There are few things more important in Our lives than Our Connections. Because of who We are, We crash and burn once in a while. And when We are fortunate to be with Our Tribe, everyone is there to pick Us up, hold Us a little if We need to cry. Maybe We pave Our way together through the struggle. But inside, there is no criticism, no assault of the senses or the heart. Inside the circle of only Us, We are safe, loved and above all, understood.

Walking with a musician

My friend Jamie O'Hara commented that while music can heal, while it can lift spirits and make a positive impact, it can also hurt, bring back unwanted memories – or in my case, take me back to somewhere I'd left so long ago.

Musicians tend to experience songs differently. When non-Musicians talk about a song, they generally talk about it as a single, fused unit: I really like/hate/wanna rip that song, man! When Musicians talk about a song, if you are fortunate enough to be in the vicinity, you will hear talk, even reverence, of fine nuances. The song's magic.

And this "insider's view" emerges when you have PTSD, because the only people who have these particular common understandings are other people who have PTSD. If you can't make all those connections, if you can't say, "Yeah, when this happens and then this happens and this happens and Bang!" then you don't get it and you sit there, you know, with a glazed look on your face and now two people are disappointed: you because you didn't get it, and Me, who tried to tell you something hoping you would you would kind of understand and make a Connection and feel closer. But it didn't happen.

You know, when you make a Connection, it's like a little tiny wall evaporates. Yeah, and it's like, it's like the wax in the beehive with all the little octagonal sections, and so it's like a wall between or around you; like you live in a little world of hexagonal boundaries and in order to make them go away, in order to see what's outside, you have to make a Connection. Because it's only the Connection that breaks the little block in the metaphor that we're using here. And when somebody doesn't get it, it's like if there were five connections, then five little blocks stay in place and it's so disappointing *because you wanted:*

You Wanted to Go There

You wanted to go there.
You wanted to see.
You wanted to know.
You wanted to feel.
You wanted to share.
You wanted to hold.

You wanted to love.

You *wanted* to do all of these things and your hopes were dashed in an instant, not because they didn't care; not because they didn't love you, but because they didn't have the experience to make the Connections.

> Together we can shift the pain into wonder and love – but it is up to us to consciously and intentionally create that connection. Sunday 8/6

The operative word here is *wanted*. When did We get the idea that We shouldn't hope to get what We want? For Me, it was when I was four and a half, three years after the traumatic Event. I was sitting on the front stoop with my grandmother. Crying. My grandmother had her arm around my tiny shoulders. She had just told Me my father had called and said he wasn't coming to see Me. A light dawned. I would never have to feel this hurt, this disappointment, if I just stopped thinking it was important to Me. And with time and the absence of emotional excitation, it became true. What I have had a hard time really grokking now is that by some mysterious process, I exorcised almost all other people too. It was the beginning of my "fun" with connection.

In talks with others, PTSD emerges along different dimensions depending on trauma source and time of Event. "Time" here refers to a combination of chronological age combined with degree of socialization. This distinction does not appear in the existing body of research. But it's important to know because otherwise people will assume that We all respond to incursions in the same way, and this is not true. Some people want a comforting arm around their shoulders; others need to be left alone so they may heal themselves. Unfortunately, it is incomprehensible to many that solitude can not only be healing, but that for some of us, it is an absolute necessity.

Resilience

I think that one of Our major characteristics is Our resilience. This is not to say that all of us are resilient all the time in every situation. But over all of these, We have cultivated the coping strategies that work for Us and these strategies are tools for managing PTSD "treats." I say it this way because using "symptoms" implies illness *a priori*, before the physical and cognitive actions, activities, and stories have been even partially understood.

Resilience in the context of PTSD research refers to Our ability to adapt to the changes that have occurred in us because of Our traumatic experiences. It is Our capacity to develop psychological well-being within the context of PTSD highs, lows, and related challenges.

What I think needs problematizing in this context is the assumption crossed with the fervent hope that We will "bounce back;" that We will "recover" Our sense of peace and happiness. The truth is that We have been changed forever and there is no going back. For me, there is no "back." I was simply too young. For those who were traumatized after being acculturated, there is a sense of "backness," a sense of there being a place that defines ways of being; ways of seeing; ways of understanding (Resilience, 2024). And since PTSD and other trauma-related exercises have been defined as *illnesses*, the popular view is that there must be a "cure."

But this is not true. First, there is no "cure;" there is only amelioration, those activities and behaviors that We use to manage Our highs, lows, and immediate responses. And intimately for Us, deeply enjoyable for others, music "soothes the savage beast."

Even for those most solidly grounded, the beast peeks out from time to time, and We beg: Please don't see Me as a monster.

Our relationships with ordinary people are very complicated and often disappointing. We don't fit their social expectations. We don't interpret social cues as expected. We don't react to social stimuli as expected. Being happy in our companionship requires developing new, more complex, more sophisticated understandings of what is "normal."

PTSD is defining a new normal. COVID-19 is responsible for ongoing PTSD in populations across the globe. Substantial ongoing research is beginning to define the shape and scope of COVID related PTSD. Research in war-torn countries such as the Ukraine is providing additional definition. New research by Velykodna (2023) has identified the connection between traumatizing experiences shared with others and a reduction in PTSD incidence and severity.

Not everyone with PTSD will make it out. Every individual is on their own path, their own journey, and each will make their own decisions about how they want to live their lives.

But those who manage through sheer force of personal will to live a full, happy and exciting life will share one characteristic: Gratitude. It's easy to complain, to blame, to wish for those times when mommy and daddy could make it better. But Posttraumatic Growth happens from the inside, literally from an intense and sustaining desire to be better.

The Vast Scope of Connections

The Connections necessary for our growth and prosperity are not limited to social encounters, but include also understanding the complexity of our physical and cognitive reactions and processes. But developing these understandings pretty much depends on whether or not We can share freely with others, free of judgements and expectations. And this takes awareness and hard work; constant attention to the myriad possibilities and opportunities available to Us because of Our special skills. It also demands that We grapple with the complex nature of Our relationships with ordinary people, those who no matter how well-meaning, will never see the inside of the sophisticated worlds that We live in.

Perhaps this is sad, but it creates a space for the development of new knowledge, new ways of being, better Connections to others and to ourselves.

 Sometimes, even the most agile of Us need help getting unstuck. Yeah, that was Me! March 1st 2024.

12: Ideas

Previous chapters often reference ideas that have been commonly known and accepted for many years. Much of this occurs because of the essential procedure in academic writing to "position oneself within the context of what researchers found and said before." This causes a promulgation of beliefs that may have been shown to be incorrect years prior but are still being held on to, ideas that no longer are very relevant within the context of current change.

Chapter 12, like the 12th musical note, completes the collection of Worlds, Spaces, Edges, Details, and the all-important Details of Edges in the topic of Understanding the Posttraumatic Mind.

Here are some of the newest findings. Findings driven by a new urgency, driven by the very frightening realization the COVID has changed the world of cognitive functioning in a way that is truly outside human ken. According to the DSM criteria, COVID-19 was the type of Event that causes PTSD, c-PTSD and their clinically ever-popular "comorbidities."

Important research coming out of war-torn Ukraine, has learned that living with a friend alleviated much of the mental stress caused by war trauma; almost all, according to the findings. (Velykodna et al. 2024). This is radically new information in a context where prior studies, way too numerous to list, have tried to link PTSD and friends to age, sex, race, and so on, without success.

Researchers Dutta & Bandyopadhyay (2024) explored Happiness as a Local Invariant of Pain: A Perspective on Spontaneous and Induced Emotions. They were specifically interested in "the intricate pathways that lead to the discovery of happiness within the realm of pain." They begin with the historical position held by psychologists and mind engineers that the positive effects of happiness would alleviate those mental states that are "characterized by suffering and pain." This characterization is the result of global tendencies to characterize, categorize, and create base behavioral templates for observable behaviors.

Behavioral templates, schemata, are a loose set of general actions. A popular example is going to a restaurant. The schema will say: arrive; park; go in; get seated; look at the menu, and so on. What Dutta & Bandyopadhyay found was that "the activation pathways of spontaneously generated emotions, driven by free will, with those induced under specific emotional states" were different. This means that the "brain" is looking at things differently in terms of configuring its expectations depending on whether it is "making up its own mind," so to speak, or whether it is mapping to a specific schema, or even several to many schemata, the interplay of which will result in new behaviors.

What this looks like for Us is that while many of those in our lives may be using one to a few schemata actively, We may have hundreds. How many has to depend hypothetically on how many stimuli we are receiving at any given time. I say hypothetically because unlike Velykodna, et al.'s finding of shared experience in symptom mediation, there is no currently published research on this specific concept.

Other important publications by van der Kolk on the immediacy of the chemical reactions, note that reaction decisions are made by the amygdala and its related structures, moving the body into action long before any cognitive interaction occurs. Serbian researchers Stanislovik, et al. (2021) discuss the major theories regarding the nature of Emotions and summarize by describing processes where Emotions are processed "bottom-up" (think fight-or-flight response and how you tell your friends about it) as different from remembering an Event, happy, sad, doesn't matter, and how you body feels when you do this. For Us, this means that We may be at the mercy of Our bodies when We empathetically receive inputs that overload Us, but also, with knowledge and skill, We can learn to play with our responses and reactions. We are Musicians. It's what We do: We take the sound from one place, dress it up, and take it out for a glorious walk in the park.

Chasing

How did we find the new neuronic connections? They had to have always been there, but mostly only as subconscious players. Then, the Trauma happens and we are shocked into disbelief, and that disbelief causes our minds to try to adjust to the forces acting upon it, one tending in one direction and one tending in the opposite direction. One direction: I can't believe this is happening; the other: Yes, it is. And the Mind will swirl around, a charred ash helix, still smoking from the flash conflagration.

And when that happens, when the Mind gives up, it can no longer guard the gates to the body's knowledge and it rains down like too much manna from heaven, overloading circuits and offering up unverifiable ideas.

My Theory

I think when we experience trauma that affects us in just the right way, we suddenly have access to the physical things our body thinks about, before the sensations come to the Cerebellum and we begin to make Feelings, and it blows our minds. We don't know what to make of it, how to handle it, and when we try to talk about it, tell someone what it's like, they tell us we're crazy

People have been taught that all Truth comes from what you can see and when we suddenly have access to the physical things our body thinks about, before the sensations come to the Cerebellum and We begin to make Feelings, and it blows Our minds. There is a scale of help available that ranges from little to none. We are stuck in a crazy-making wasteland that only We have the capability to understand, to manage. We don't have the necessary language or shared experiences to connect with those whose brains are ordinary, those who haven't been through the traumatic experiences that have changed Us so permanently and dramatically.

Yeah. PTSD changes us, remember? Actually, it's not the PTSD. It's the traumatic Event. The physical trauma. The emotional trauma. Something so awful it would be beyond the ability of each unique individual to imagine it. And that's why they can't predict who based on the parameters that work for medical research. It's because the reaction to the trauma is Fucking Unique to Each Individual's Brain Space.

The following scene takes place in a hotel "in one of the most lawless countries in the planet" (p. 72). Two high-ranking intelligence officers, one American, one British, are interrogating the missing analyst. There has been an "impossible" intelligence leak and no one can figure out how. Clearly, there is not a lot of hard data available. The suspect says "I couldn't help feeling that Dave was somehow involved." (Archer & Banner, 2024, p. 75).

The missing analyst's "feeling" has to be the result of information coming upwards from his body; his body, subconsciously in this case, responding to something unusual in Dave's vibrations. This is a vague feeling, not grounded in analysis, hence not a product of top-down, cerebral initiation.

The Final Countdown

Given the wide range of historical theories, I feel safe in presenting how I see it from a lifetime of learning and coping, learning more and coping. We have access to three main "parts" and who We are is a function of Our often unique ability to process across Our parts: Emotions (body); Feelings (Cerebellum); Story (Cerebrum). It's generalized, but it works. The general idea in a management style that works is: Avoid the rush to judgment. That is, don't make Story until you have more of or the full picture.

I decide what to do by listening to your voice. It goes right through my body and together they tell me what I need to know, even if they have already done the action.

The Review Page: Was It Good?

Hey it's AJ

If you believe in the book and what it's saying, please share what you feel in an Amazon review.

I know it's called a "review" but this isn't about selling. It's about getting the sound out to the people who want to hear it.

Here's the link: Do It Now☺. Jump on it and do your thing with the book and then do something: Call your friends; write a great review about You. It really is all about you, you know.

Then check out Randy's or Alison's or Paul's music.

warm hugs, AJ

P.S. I thought you might like to see how I might write a review

A small child: and then what happened?

What happened is it truly hellacious rocking ride to Freedom as AJ and her friends in the Las Cruces music community share stories poetry and song lyrics.

"Healing is a sound..." Laura Bressan

If you read the book, you'll know that Aj is the real deal. As Aly is fond of saying, You can't make this stuff up.

If the book helped you, pay it forward and tell everyone. If it didn't, still pay it forward and tell everyone. Do It Now☺

Glossary

CBT (Cognitive Behavioral Therapy): A type of talk therapy that teaches people new ways of thinking to handle different problems.

Coping Mechanisms: The methods used by individuals to deal with stressful situations.

DBT (Dialectical Behavior Therapy): A type of cognitive-behavioral therapy that teaches behavioral skills to help handle stress, manage emotions, and improve relationships.

Derealization: A feeling that the external world is unfamiliar or unreal.

Dissociation: A mental process of disconnecting from one's feelings, thoughts, memories, or sense of inclusion in the physical world.

Distress Tolerance: An individual's ability to manage actual or perceived emotional distress.

EMDR (Eye Movement Desensitization and Reprocessing): A form of psychotherapy that helps people heal from the symptoms of traumatic events.

Emotional Regulation: The ability to manage and respond to an experiencing emotional state effectively.

Flashback: Sudden, powerful re-experience of a past event.

Flashbacks: Sudden, vivid, intense recollections of past traumatic events. (Both of these are here because it can be both a recollection OR a re-experience. It is critically important to understand the difference between simply remembering, here "recollecting" an event and re-experiencing, literally reliving that event)

fMRI: One of the biggest disadvantages has to do with fMRI scan timing vs. how fast your brain works. An fMRI captures scan data from second to second. Brain activity changes in tiny fractions of a second, so fMRI can't scan fast enough to capture very detailed brain activity. May 27, 2023. Retrieved 10/11/2023 from https://my.clevelandclinic.org/health/diagnostics/25034-functional-mri-fmri

Grounding: A technique used to bring attention back to the present moment during a flashback.

Hypervigilance: Enhanced state of sensory sensitivity prompted by expectation of danger.

Intrusions: Unwanted, often repetitious thoughts related to the trauma.

Meditation: A practice that uses mindfulness or focusing the mind on a particular object, thought or activity to train attention and awareness.

Mindfulness: The practice of being fully present and engaged in the current moment.

MRI: Magnetic resonance imaging (MRI) is a type of scan that uses strong magnetic fields and radio waves to produce detailed images of the inside of the body. Retrieved 10/11/2023 from https://www.nhs.uk/conditions/mri-scan/#:~:text=Magnetic%20resonance%20imaging%20(MRI)%20is,the%20tube%20during%20the%20scan.

Psychiatrist: A doctor who specializes in mental health, primarily with the use of prescription drugs.

PTG (Post-traumatic growth): Positive psychological change experienced as a result of adversity and other challenges.

PTSD (Post-Traumatic Stress Disorder): A psychiatric disorder that occurs in people who have experienced or witnessed a traumatic event.

Recovery: The process of becoming or making something become healthy after illness or trauma.

Resilience: Ability to bounce back from adversity, trauma, tragedy, threats, stress, disappointment, and failure.

Somatic Therapy: A form of body-centered therapy that helps individuals to release trapped trauma through physical experiences.

Support Group: A gathering of people who share common experiences or problems and provide each other with encouragement, comfort, and advice.

Trauma Bonding: A strong emotional attachment between an abused person and their abuser, formed as a result of the cycle of violence.

Traumatic Break: term for the kind of "breaches of control" that We monitor and attempt to control. So if the time-honored tradition of new ideas everywhere. Since I couldn't find a word to describe precisely what I mean here, I created a word to say what I mean.

References

AMKC, n.d. Affective Musical Key Characteristics. https://wmich.edu/mustheo/courses/keys.html. Translated from the original source: Steblin, R. (1983). A History of Key Characteristics in the 18th and Early 19th Centuries: Second Edition. (Retrieved 9th, 2023).

Archer, D., Banner, B. (2024). Blood on Megiddo, Kindle Version, p. 75.

Britannica, T. Editors of Encyclopaedia (2023, September 20). Eric Clapton. Encyclopedia Britannica. https://www.britannica.com/biography/Eric-Clapton.

Broekman, B., Olff, M., Boer, F. (2007). *The genetic background to PTSD*. Neuroscience & Biobehavioral Reviews 31 (3), 348-362, 2007.

Costandi, M. Neuroplasticity. (2016).

D'Andrea, W., Pole, N., DePierro, J., Steven Freed, S., D., and, Wallace, B. (2013). *Heterogeneity of defensive responses after exposure to trauma: Blunted autonomic reactivity in response to startling sounds*, International Journal of Psychophysiology, Volume 90, Issue 1,2013, Pages 80-89, ISSN 0167-8760, https://doi.org/10.1016/j.ijpsycho.2013.07.008.(https://www.sciencedirect.com/science/article/pii/S016787601300216X)

Damasio, A.R. (2004). *Emotions and Feelings*. Feelings and emotions: The Amsterdam symposium 5, 49-57, 2004.

Day, R.A. and Thompson, W.F. (2019) *Measuring the onset of experiences of emotion and imagery in response to music.* Psychomusicology 29, 75–89

Diagnostic and Statistical Manual of Mental Disorders, Third Edition. (1980). American Psychiatric Association, P. 236, Section 309.81

Diagnostic and Statistical Manual of Mental Disorders, Fifth Edition. (1980). American Psychiatric Association, P. 271, Section 309.81

Eagleman, D.M., Tse, P.U., Buonomano, D., Peter Janssen, P., Nobre, A.C., and, Holcombe, A.O. (2005). *Time and the Brain: How Subjective Time Relates to Neural Time.* The Journal of Neuroscience, November 9, 2005, 25(45):10369–10371

Eames, T. 2022. The tragic story of Marvin Gaye and the untimely death of a soul legend. retrieved 11/23/2023 from https://www.smoothradio.com/artists/marvin-gaye/marvin-gaye-death-father-explained/#:~:text=Marvin%20reportedly%20suffered%20the%20worst,and%20all%2Dpowerful%20king%22. April 1, 2022.

Friedman, B.H. (2010). *Feelings and the body: the Jamesian perspective on autonomic specificity of emotion.* Biol Psychol. 2010 Jul;84(3):383-93. doi: 10.1016/j.biopsycho.2009.10.006. Epub 2009 Oct 29. PMID: 19879320.

Janiri, D., Carfì, A., Kotzalidis, G.D., Bernabei, R., Landi, F., Sani, G., Gemelli. (2021). Against COVID, Post-Acute Care Study Group. *Posttraumatic stress disorder in patients after severe COVID-19 infection.* JAMA psychiatry 78 (5), 567-569, 2021.

Jasiewicz, K., Roos, H., Davies, N., Dawson, A. H., Wandycz, P. S., Smogorzewski, K. M., & Kondracki, J. A. (2024, February 12). Poland | History, Flag, Map, Population, President, Religion, & Facts. Encyclopedia Britannica. https://www.britannica.com/place/Poland Retrieved 10/11/2023.

Kirkland, P. (2023). Burning Evidence. Kindle Unlimited. P. 45.

Koelsch, S. (2010). *Towards a neural basis of music-evoked emotions.* Trends Cogn Sci. 2010 Mar;14(3):131-7.

Krystal, J.H., Abdallah, C.G., Averill, L.A. (2017). *Synaptic Loss and the Pathophysiology of PTSD: Implications for Ketamine as a Prototype Novel Therapeutic.* Curr Psychiatry Rep 19, 74 (2017). https://doi.org/10.1007/s11920-017-0829-z

Liyanage-Don, N.A., Winawer, M. R., Hamberger, M. J., Agarwal, S., Trainor, A. R., Kristal A. Quispe, K.A., and, Kronish, I.M. (2022) *Association of depression and COVID-induced PTSD with cognitive symptoms after COVID-19 illness.* General Hospital Psychiatry, Volume 76, 2022, Pages 45-48, ISSN 0163-8343, https://doi.org/10.1016/j.genhosppsych.2022.02.006.(https://www.sciencedirect.com/science/article/pii/S016383432200024X)

McCormick, K. (2017). Dragon Colors: White Dragons. Retrieved from https://www.blackdrago.com/colors_white.htm#:~:text=A%20solar%2Dwhite%20dragon%20is,dragon%20symbolizes%20death%20and%20rebirth December 26, 2023.

McDowell, E. (2023). Em & Friends Finding Yourself Journal. Retrieved from: https://emandfriends.com/products/finding-yourself-journal, November 3, 2023.

Mechling, L. September 15, 2021. *The Silver Era of Andie McDowell.* TZR: The Zoe Report. Retrieved online from https://www.thezoereport.com/culture/andie-macdowell-maid-gray-hair-hollywood, retrieved November 27, 2023.

MPP Digital Team. (2020). Stevie Wonder – Singer & Songwriter. Retrieved March 7th, 2024, from https://musicplaypatrol.com/2020/11/kindergarten-5th-grade-stevie-wonder/#:~:text=Stevie%20Wonder%20has%20been%20blind,ever%20to%20top%20the%20chart.

Nichols, D.E. & Nichols, C. D. (2008). *serotonin receptors*. Chemical reviews 108 (5), 1614-1641, 2008.

Office of the Historian. (2019). A Guide to the United States' History of Recognition, Diplomatic, and Consular Relations, by Country, since 1776: Poland. Retrieved from https://history.state.gov/countries/poland#:~:text=Poland%20vanished%20from%20the%20map,proclaimed%20on%20November%203%2C%201918. 10/11/2023.

Priebe, K., Kleindienst, N., Schropp, A., Dyer, A., Krüger-Gottschalk, A., Schmahl, C., Steil, R., and Bohusa, M. (2018). *Defining the index trauma in post-traumatic stress disorder patients with multiple trauma exposure: impact on severity scores and treatment effects of using worst single incident versus multiple traumatic events*. European Journal of Psychotraumatology. 9(1): 1486124. Published online 2018 Jul 9. doi: 10.1080/20008198.2018.1486124 PMCID: PMC6052424PMID: 30034640

Rasmussen, A. February 9, 2023.Bad Blood' Between Marvin Gaye And His Father Led To Motown Legend's Murder. Retrieved from: https://www.investigationdiscovery.com/crimefeed/celebrity/bad-blood-between-marvin-gaye-and-his-father-led-to-motown-legends-murder, 11/24/2023.

Resilience. (2024, February 8). Merriam-Webster Dictionary. https://www.merriam-webster.com/dictionary/resilience

Sedikides, C., Wildschut, T., Routledge, C., Arndt, J., Hepper, E.G., Zhou, X. (2015). *Chapter Five – To Nostalgize: Mixing Memory with Affect and Desire*, Editor(s): James M. Olson, Mark P. Zanna, Advances in Experimental Social Psychology, Academic Press, Volume 51, 2015, Pages 189-273. ISSN 0065-2601, ISBN 9780128022740, https://doi.org/10.1016/bs.aesp.2014.10.001. (https://www.sciencedirect.com/science/article/pii/S0065260114000045)

Seligowski, A.V., Lebois, L.A.M., Hill, S.B., Kahhale, I., Wolff, J.D., Jovanovic, T., Winternitz, S.R., Kaufman, M.L., Ressler, K.J. (2019).*Oh oh Autonomic responses to fear conditioning among women with PTSD and dissociation*. Depress Anxiety. 2019 Jul;36(7):625-634. doi: 10.1002/da.22903. Epub 2019 Apr 22. PMID: 31012207; PMCID: PMC6602841

Simmons, R., Singhal, N., Sullivan, J., Shih, T., Tihan, T., Poduri, A., Smith, L., Yang, E. (2023). *Epilepsy surgery as a treatment option for select patients with PCDH19-related epilepsy*, Epilepsy & Behavior, Volume 149, 2023, 109517. ISSN

1525-5050, https://doi.org/10.1016/j.yebeh.2023.109517. (https://www.sciencedirect.com/science/article/pii/S1525505023004365)

Stanley, P. (2014). Face the Music: A Life Exposed, Kindle Edition. HarperOne.

Stone, M., Rhodes, L. (2023) Shadow's Mystery. Mary Stone Publishing.

photomicrograph. (n.d.). Merriam-Webster Dictionary. https://www.merriam-webster.com/dictionary/photomicrograph Accessed 11 Oct. 2023.

Taku, K, Cann A, Calhoun LG, Tedeschi RG. (2008). *The factor structure of the posttraumatic growth inventory: a comparison of five models using confirmatory factor analysis.* J Trauma Stress. 2008 Apr;21(2):158-64. doi: 10.1002/jts.20305. PMID: 18404631

Tedeschi, R., Calhoun, L., and Grolieu, J.M. (2015). *Clinical Applications of Posttraumatic Growth.* P. 503-508. In Positive Psychology in Practice: Promoting Human Flourishing in Work, Health, Education, and Everyday Life. Stephen Joseph (Ed.). 2015, John Wiley & Sons.

Toof, J., Wong, J., Devlin, J.M. (2020). *Childhood trauma and attachment.* The Family Journal 28 (2), 194-198, 2020.

Torrey, F.; Simmons, W.W.; and, Dailey, L. 2023. *The NIMH Research Portfolio: An Update.* August 1, 2023. Prim Care Companion CNS Disord 2023;25(4):23m03486

van der Kolk, B. (2015). The Body Keeps Score. Penguin Books.

Velykodna, M., Charyieva, O., Kvitka, N., Mitchenko, K., Shylo, O., Tkachenko, O.

(2024). *Living with a friend mediates PTSD and CPTSD symptoms among trauma-exposed Ukrainians during the second year of 2022 Russian invasion.* Mental Health and Social Inclusion. 9 January 2024.

Wisco, B.E., Marx, B.P., Wolf, E.J., Miller, M.W., Southwick, S.M., Pietrzak, R.H. (2014) Posttraumatic stress disorder in the US veteran population: Results from the National Health and Resilience in Veterans Study.

Wisdom Living 101. (2023) Lady Gaga on Mental Health Part 1. Available at: https://youtube.com/watch?v=MvJdh-dg5Sc&si=pyeubKjnHjvEQ7y8.

Wolframe, P. M. (2013). *The Madwoman in the Academy, or, Revealing the Invisible Straightjacket: Theorizing and Teaching Saneism and Sane Privilege.* Disability Studies Quarterly. Vol. 33 No. 1 (2013).

Index

A

ADHD 12
Alex 9
Alison Reynolds 8, 9, 84, 86
Aly 9, 47, 72, 73, 75, 87, 89, 121
Alzheimer's Disease 67
amelioration 125
Andie McDowell 51
anguish 89
Archer 130, 135
Aristotle 102
art 89, 104
Autism Spectrum Disorders 67
Avoidance of Triggers 27

B

Back to You 84
bassplayer 86
Bobby 9, 41, 71, 72
Brain 14, 32, 34, 38, 45, 48, 92, 130, 133, 135
breaches of control 15, 134
Britannica 30, 135, 136
Broekman 102, 135

C

Calhoun 59, 60, 61, 138
ChatGPT 16, 29, 55, 62, 68, 102, 118
Chuck Sutherland 9, 118
Clarity 86
Connection 16, 124
cure 20, 102, 114, 125

D

D'Andrea 35, 135
Damasio 120, 135
Dave Ferris 84
David Bowie 59
Day 59, 135
Diagnostic and Statistical Manual of Mental Disorders 27, 135
doctors
    Aristotle 102
    Galen 102
dogged determination 89, 105
DSM 4, 27, 28, 31, 34, 58, 60, 128
DSM-5-TR 27

E

Eames 52, 135
emotion 58, 86, 99, 114, 135, 136
Emotional instability 26
emotional memories 92
Epilepsy 68, 137
Event ... 15, 32, 34, 39, 45, 46, 48, 75, 77, 90, 91, 96, 97, 124, 125, 128, 129, 130
Events 25, 45, 48, 60, 72, 86, 88, 90, 97, 103, 105

F

Face the Music 13, 57, 138
father's language 117
feelings 12, 20, 32, 56, 58, 65, 76, 78, 86, 92, 94, 102, 105, 106, 133
Feelings 45, 48, 56, 59, 90, 91, 92, 93, 95, 101, 105, 120, 130, 131, 135, 136
Flashbacks 14, 44, 68, 133

fMRI 97, 133
Frequent Sadness 26
Friedman 97, 136

G

Grolieu 61, 138
ground 17, 39, 40, 65, 86, 116, 121
guilt 27, 76, 89

H

hairTriggers 27
heart 18, 35, 41, 57, 58, 68, 89, 99, 105, 110, 112, 123
heart 13, 16, 17
Hope 16, 69
Hypervigilance 45, 91, 133

I

I Am Just A Boy 13
I Was Made For Loving You 13
illnesses 27, 125

J

Jamie O'Hara 8, 9, 81, 123
Janiri 25, 136
Jasiewicz 30, 136
Jim Rendon 60
journey 22, 47, 84, 85, 110

K

Keanu Reeves 12
Kirkland 136
Krystal 67, 68, 136

L

Lady Gaga 51, 138

Laura Bressan 9, 106, 132
Liam 9, 121, 122
Lou Reed 58

M

Magic 88, 89, 90, 95, 96, 100
Marvin Gaye 51, 135, 137
McDowell 136
Mechling 51, 136
memories 21, 28, 44, 73, 76, 91, 93, 123, 133
Mind ... 14, 24, 28, 31, 32, 34, 35, 36, 38, 41, 44, 45, 48, 51, 52, 53, 61, 90, 129, 130
monocausal mental disorder 28
MPP Digital Team 117, 136
MRI 97, 134
music... 12, 13, 15, 41, 43, 49, 51, 54, 58, 73, 78, 81, 89, 95, 104, 107, 110, 111, 112, 113, 121, 122, 123, 125, 135, 136
Musicians . 12, 51, 54, 78, 104, 105, 123, 129

N

Neural Pathways 102
neurophysiologists
    Broca 102
    McLean 102
    Papez 102
Nichols 93, 137
normal 19, 25, 26, 27, 36, 68, 90, 93, 108, 126

O

OCD 12
Office of the Historian 30, 137
ordinary people 54, 71, 82, 101, 126
Orrin (O.B.) Wayland 9, 78
    Pictures 78

P

pain 13, 17, 19, 28, 32, 48, 49, 58, 62, 66, 73, 76, 77, 89, 95, 121, 128

Parkinson's Disease 68
Paul Stanley 13, 16, 57
Paul Walter Kimball 9, 81, 84
personal strength 89
philosophers
    Aristotle 102
philosophers
    Plato 102
philosophers
    Spinoza 102
philosophers
    Descartes 102
Posttraumatic Growth 22, 42, 56, 60, 89, 126, 138
Posttraumatic Mind 128
Priebe 98, 137
PTG 134
PTGers 12
PTSD 11, 12, 13, 14, 15, 16, 17, 18, 19, 20, 21, 22, 24, 25, 26, 27, 29, 31, 32, 34, 35, 36, 37, 38, 41, 42, 51, 54, 59, 60, 61, 62, 67, 68, 69, 88, 89, 90, 92, 95, 96, 97, 98, 99, 102, 118, 120, 121, 122, 123, 125, 126, 128, 130, 134, 135, 136, 137, 138

R

Randy Lynch 8, 9, 75, 88
Reality 102, 109
Recollection of Past Trauma 27
relationship 75, 76, 78, 88
Relationships 27
Research ... 12, 15, 22, 26, 35, 36, 61, 93, 96, 97, 98, 99, 126, 138
Research Community 12
Resilience 125, 134, 137, 138

rewards 96
Rhythm 86

S

Schizophrenia 67
Seligowski 35, 137
shivers 80
shut-up-ation 45
Simmons 68, 137, 138
social cues 126
social expectations 126
Stan Eisen 13
Stanislovik 102, 129
Stanley 11, 60, 138
Stone 138
Story 45, 48, 59, 70, 75, 79, 90, 91, 95, 97, 102, 103, 104, 118, 119, 131
symptoms 22, 34, 35, 61, 68, 69, 84, 114, 125, 133, 136, 138
synaptopathies 67, 68

T

Tauna Cole-Dorn 8, 9
Tedeschi 59, 60, 61, 62, 138
The Literature 26
The Starchild 9, 13, 57, 60
Tim McKellar 84
Too Long Sober 76
Toof 55, 138
touch 12, 20, 35, 37, 43, 59, 85, 113
transformation 89
transformations 80, 104
Trauma Bonding 134
Trauma Event 15
Traumatic Break 15, 134
treats 96, 125

Tribe 12, 15, 16, 21, 123

V

Validation 50
van der Kolk 129, 138
Velykodna 37, 126, 128, 129, 138
Veterans 15, 69, 138
vocabulary 88

W

What Is Trauma 27
White Dragon 95, 96
Who am I 12, 49, 86, 87
Wisdom Living 101 .... 51, 138
world view 26

Y

Yellow
    Orrin (O.B.) Wayland 78

www.ingramcontent.com/pod-product-compliance
Lightning Source LLC
Chambersburg PA
CBHW060509030426
42337CB00015B/1818